MW00450602

# Praise for *The Big Turnaround*

Ellen offers an insightful, behind-the-scenes peek into the things that can go wrong in a small business, especially when a leadership transition isn't managed well. This book emphasizes that understanding what went wrong in the first place is key to being able to come up with viable options when making changes, whether you have people problems or process problems.

Patricia Duggan, The Duggan Difference, LLC

McIlhenny has put her finger on the insidious dysfunctions that plague many businesses today. Fear, ego, and cronyism conspire to nearly bring Burgess Industries to its knees but, through the implementation of sound management practices and tough decision making, the company is able to rebound and thrive. Unlike many business books, *The Big Turnaround* is chock full of practical, actionable insights that business executives should apply today to grow their companies and to create lasting value.

Michael Metzger

*Certified Business Intermediary, Murphy Business Sales*

Thank you, Ellen McIlhenny, for sharing this story and its vivid characters. It's an instructive business book with the page-turning intrigue of a suspense novel.

Todd Bradberry, MBA

*CEO, Parallel Management Company*

This modern-day parable will ring true with senior leaders. Through Darcy, we see the signs and symptoms of the embedded issues that plague businesses across all industries. This compelling story will help you see your business in a new light. Ellen McIlhenny has delivered a gem!

**Robin Green**
*President, Sandler Training, Richmond, VA*


From the first chapter, this book gives you a real sense of the characters and factors at play. You quickly understand what motivates the team and are able to see from the inside the issues that the business is facing.

**Alison Conners**
*President, Executive Forums of Virginia*

HOW **BAD MANAGEMENT** NEARLY
DESTROYED AN **EXCEPTIONAL COMPANY**

# THE BIG
# TURNAROUND

ELLEN McILHENNY

*Advantage*®

Published by Advantage, Charleston, South Carolina.
Member of Advantage Media Group.

ADVANTAGE is a registered trademark, and the Advantage colophon is a trademark of Advantage Media Group, Inc.

Printed in the United States of America.

10  9  8  7  6  5  4  3  2  1

ISBN: 978-1-64225-017-6
LCCN: 2018939813

Cover design by Melanie Cloth.
Layout design by Megan Elger.

This publication is designed to provide accurate and authoritative information in regard to the subject matter covered. It is sold with the understanding that the publisher is not engaged in rendering legal, accounting, or other professional services. If legal advice or other expert assistance is required, the services of a competent professional person should be sought.

Advantage Media Group is proud to be a part of the Tree Neutral® program. Tree Neutral offsets the number of trees consumed in the production and printing of this book by taking proactive steps such as planting trees in direct proportion to the number of trees used to print books. To learn more about Tree Neutral, please visit **www.treeneutral.com.**

Advantage Media Group is a publisher of business, self-improvement, and professional development books and online learning. We help entrepreneurs, business leaders, and professionals share their Stories, Passion, and Knowledge to help others Learn & Grow. Do you have a manuscript or book idea that you would like us to consider for publishing? Please visit **advantagefamily.com** or call **1.866.775.1696.**

*To my guys: Dennis, Ben, Woody, and CW—the loves of my life.*

# TABLE OF CONTENTS

FOREWORD . . . . . . . . . . . . . . . . . . . . . . . . . . . . . . . xi

PREFACE . . . . . . . . . . . . . . . . . . . . . . . . . . . . . . . . xiii

1. CHANGE . . . . . . . . . . . . . . . . . . . . . . . . . . . . . 1

2. CALM BEFORE THE STORM . . . . . . . . . . . . . . . . 9

3. AMBUSH . . . . . . . . . . . . . . . . . . . . . . . . . . . . . 19

4. A WAY OUT? . . . . . . . . . . . . . . . . . . . . . . . . . . 27

5. A NEW DIRECTION . . . . . . . . . . . . . . . . . . . . . 33

6. DARYL THE DISRUPTOR . . . . . . . . . . . . . . . . . 37

7. A WAY OUT (PART 2) . . . . . . . . . . . . . . . . . . . . 49

8. THE SMT . . . OR IS IT THE SLT? . . . . . . . . . . . . . 55

9. WHOSE CORE VALUES? . . . . . . . . . . . . . . . . . 67

10. COMMUNITY OUTREACH . . . . . . . . . . . . . . . . 79

11. THE NEW DIGS . . . . . . . . . . . . . . . . . . . . . . . 89

12. ENOUGH IS ENOUGH . . . . . . . . . . . . . . . . . . 101

13. MAPPING THE ROAD TO RECOVERY . . . . . . . 115

14. THE BIG TURNAROUND . . . . . . . . . . . . . . . . . . . . 149

EPILOGUE. . . . . . . . . . . . . . . . . . . . . . . . . . . . . . . . . 155

ABOUT THE AUTHOR. . . . . . . . . . . . . . . . . . . . . . . . 161

# FOREWORD

**I have known Ellen** since December 8, 1980, when we went on a blind date set up by Margaret Johnston, her friend and Sigma Kappa sorority sister at Virginia Tech.

Ellen is an amazing woman, both personally and professionally. Together we have three boys. We were challenged early when our first son, Ben, was born with developmental disabilities and Cerebral Palsy. We rose to the situation and became a stronger couple because of our son's special needs. Ellen became an advocate and activist in the special needs community. She has held positions on several non-profit boards, is the author of the blog www.tri9mom.com, and served two years as the chairman of the State Rehabilitation Council for the Commonwealth of Virginia. Our middle son, Woody, much to our pleasure, is an undergraduate at Virginia Tech, and will hopefully be followed by his younger brother, CW.

Ellen has over thirty years of experience as a CFO and business manager. She has managed the due diligence in multiple acquisitions. She has seen firsthand what can go wrong and how to make it right to benefit of the business owner. Ellen has been the boss and has worked for both good and bad bosses. Currently, she is a partner with a strategic CFO firm, consulting with her clients on how to best put their fiscal houses in order to maximize the value of their companies.

Her book, *The Big Turnaround*, is unique because it is a business novel, not your normal 'how-to' or dry business book. It illustrates in an entertaining way the good, the bad, and the ugly business lessons of management that Ellen has lived and seen in her career. The reader will benefit from an imaginative illustration of business tips and tricks of the interactions of business management all leading to a happy ending.

**Dennis D. McIlhenny**
Husband to Ellen
Father to Ben, Woody, and CW

# PREFACE

**After many attempts at starting** to write but never completing a book, the concept for *The Big Turnaround* came to me in October 2017 and was written in one month during November 2017 for National Novel Writing Month (NANOWRIMO). In preparation, I took a long look at the thirty-plus years of my career during which I worked for other people. I wanted to illustrate areas of concern that might be especially helpful for business owners, and I felt that the novel format would be an easier and more enjoyable read than your standard business book. I used the office products industry only because that is what I know best, having spent most of my career there, though the issues dealt with in this book are by no means unique to that industry. The characters in this book are composites of people I have either worked with or have known of— all were flawed in some way, and all contributed to the downfall of Burgess Industries. Bob Burgess, the owner, chooses to ignore the red flags rather than leave his comfort zone. Ron Marchetti, Bob's hand-picked successor, has trust issues and a need to be in total control. The rest of the management team for a long time takes the path of least resistance rather than challenge the status quo. All of the players are equally at fault for the problems the company faces after Bob retires. I hope that one take-away for you as a reader will be that no one person has all the right answers. It takes teamwork, trust, and communication to build a truly great company.

I had so much fun writing this book that I have already come up with an idea for the prequel. During my career, both as a CFO and a consultant, I have encountered several small business owners who are ready to sell; some more desperate than others. As with Burgess, there are often a lot of issues within the business that need to be addressed to maximize value prior to selling. My thought is to explore Burgess' experience in buying businesses and some of the challenges that Darcy Holtzman, Burgess's CFO, has to confront while performing the due diligence in preparation for their purchase transactions. My hope will be that I'm able to convince business owners that there is no better time than now to plan for the day they leave the company, whether that day is soon or far in the future. As I tell the many business owners I talk to, the only sure things in life are death, taxes, and … transitioning out of your company (whether it is planned or unplanned).

Thanks for reading, and I hope you enjoy *The Big Turnaround*.

# CHANGE

**After fourteen exciting years,** the ride was going to be over just as quickly as it started. Darcy Holtzman stared at Bob Burgess in disbelief, not quite knowing how to comprehend what she had just heard. Darcy had been Bob's chief financial officer and advisor on other personal financial matters during a period of dramatic growth for Bob's company. Through both acquisition and organic growth, Bob had transformed his company into the largest independent office products dealership in all of North Carolina. He was now sitting across from her saying that he was tired, and though he had no plans to sell right now, he was going to step down as the president and leader of Burgess Industries. Effective immediately, Ronald Marchetti, the current chief operating officer, would take over as president.

"Darcy, you will take on the role of senior vice president and chief financial officer. I'd like you to take over some of the areas of operations that Ron has been heading up. Of course, it will mean more money," Bob said in a matter of fact tone.

At that moment, Darcy knew she was at a disadvantage. It was obvious from the moment she sat down at the conference room table with Bob and Ron that she was the only one hearing this news for the first time. One thing Darcy hated was being blindsided. It took every ounce of control not to show the rising anger and hurt she felt at that moment. She and Bob had been friends for many years, long before he had asked her to come and work for him fourteen years earlier. At first, she had done it more as a favor than anything. The company was strangled by cash flow issues, and there was no accounting department to speak of—Darcy had to start from scratch. She thought about how it all began. When she started at Burgess Industries, Bob's wife, Jill, was still paying the bills. Jill would send a batch of checks to the office each week, and, because there was no money in the bank, Darcy would stick them in a drawer. Darcy would send the most important checks out as money came in from customers. Those really were the "salad days." Though there was a lot of stress, they all had so much fun striving for success within the company and watching it flourish. In the process, they became a family. Now, everything was going to change.

"Darcy, can I get your thoughts?" Bob asked, noticing the look of shock on her face.

"Wow, Bob, that's quite a surprise. You can have my thoughts, but it sounds like the decision is made, isn't it?" At this point, Darcy was doing everything in her power to contain herself.

"Well, yeah, but I'd still like to know what you think," said Bob. He was beginning to realize he made a big mistake not talking to Darcy alone prior to this meeting.

"First, Ron I can't tell you how happy I am for you. You must be quite honored to be asked to take over such a great company." Ron smiled and nodded with just a hint of surprise. He had been sure that Darcy would completely lose it. He had not been in favor of breaking the news to her in this way, but Bob had insisted. Bob avoided conflict whenever possible, and he knew Darcy well enough to know that she would not cause a big scene with Ron in the room.

Darcy continued, "Second, I wish you both the best of luck. Ron, my resignation will be on your desk by the end of the day." *Did I just say that?* she thought to herself, but she couldn't tell who looked more surprised at her words, Ron or Bob.

"Now hold on Darcy. Let's not do anything drastic," Bob blurted out. "You really should take some time to contemplate what you're doing. Shouldn't you at least talk this over with Jimmy?" Jimmy was Darcy's husband of twenty-five years, as well as a longtime friend of Bob's.

"Bob, the truth is, Jimmy and I have been talking about it. Recently, since I've had so much trouble getting you to even discuss my salary, Jimmy recommended that I reach out to someone who approached me about a business opportunity last year. I did, and it sounds very promising. Until today I haven't wanted to leave, but you just gave me a good reason to do it."

At this point, Ron weighed in. "Darcy, this is going to be something very new to me, and I need your help. Losing you right now would really hurt the company. I know very little about what you do and how your department works. I'm begging you not to leave."

Darcy wanted to scream. Ron's plea was so disingenuous. This was a guy who didn't need anyone. It was true that he knew nothing about her department, but that did not mean he wouldn't try to control her every move. She immediately dismissed Ron and looked at Bob.

"Bob, I'm going to be completely honest right now. I can't stay because I could never work for Ron. You see, I don't exactly agree with his management style. Ron is a micromanager to the nth degree and, as you know, my managers need the freedom to run the department as they see fit. That just won't happen with Ron. I have built that department from nothing, and I'll be damned if I let anyone try to change it on my watch."

Darcy stopped and looked at both Ron and Bob sitting across from her. Ron's face was beet-red. She wasn't sure if it was from embarrassment or anger, but if she had to guess, she would pick the latter.

Bob's look was sullen. It never even occurred to him that she would quit. She was as integral a part of the company as anyone. He couldn't imagine it without her. He realized at that moment he was going to have to go way outside of his comfort zone and try to fix this. He hated these kinds of conversations. Hell, that's what he had Ron for. Ron seemed to relish this kind of stuff—except when he was the topic of conversation.

Ron had been working with Bob even longer than Darcy. Twenty-five years earlier, he was a young salesperson working for Bob, who at that time was the sales manager at another local dealership. When Bob decided to go out on his own, he recruited a few of his most loyal employees—Ron was tapped to be his sales manager. Bob taught Ron everything he knew about the business and, in return, he earned Ron's undying loyalty. However, there were two things that

Bob was unable to teach Ron: how to be a visionary, and how to be a leader.

Over the years, Bob chose to ignore most of the complaints he received about Ron's treatment of his employees. By now the complaints had virtually stopped. Not because the situation was better, but because nothing was ever done to fix it. Employees either resigned themselves to working for someone who gave them no authority and blamed them for everything that went wrong, or they quit. Eventually, almost all ended up quitting.

"Okay, let's try to come up with a solution to this," said Bob, trying to clear the air in the room. The tension between Ron and Darcy could have been cut with a knife.

"I believe I have already done that," said Darcy, a little too smug. "The truth is, Bob, I just don't see Ron and me working together in any way that would be beneficial to the company."

There was a long silence. Finally, Ron took a deep breath and said, "Listen, Darcy, I realize I can be a bit of a control freak at times. My wife wants to kill me most of the time. However, just because you'll now be working for me, I really don't see much changing. Except I would like your input when you want to give it. You've shown that you can run an effective department. Why would I change that? I'll transition the new departments over to you, and I'll let you run them as you see fit."

Darcy looked at Ron skeptically. She didn't trust him as far as she could throw him. He was famous for bending the truth to get what he wanted. She had to hand it to him, though: he was a master of the art of persuasion, and had a knack for convincing disgruntled employees who were ready to leave the company to forgive all his past transgressions. They would come out of the meetings convinced that things would be different going forward, only to find out it was all a ruse. At some point, Ron would fall back into his old habits. She could feel herself falling into the same trap as she began to think about what it would be like to have the additional departments under her wing. The money wouldn't hurt, either. What harm would it do to try? She could always leave later if it didn't work out.

Bob could see that Darcy's demeanor was softening a bit. "Come on, Darcy. Please try this for me. I'll only be a phone call away if you need to talk. Oh, and I forgot to mention: in addition to the added responsibility and money, with this new position you'll both become officers of the company. There will also be a couple of substantial insurance policies written on me with the two of you as beneficiaries. If anything happens to me, both of you will get a very large payout which I hope you will use to buy the company from my estate. Heaven knows Jill and the kids won't want anything to do with it." At that, Darcy tried to imagine herself as Ron's business partner. She knew that would never happen.

"Listen, I know I'm going to sell the company when the right buyer comes along. You know, we've talked about this before. I need a buyer who wants to preserve and grow the company in its current state. I really do want to protect the employees. When that time comes along, I want you to know that I plan to take care of you both." Bob had made this statement before, and it always prompted Darcy to wonder what "taking care of them" really meant. However, she wasn't terribly concerned with it, because Bob had tested the waters a few times over the years, but had only come close to selling once. Darcy's thought was that Bob's perception of the worth of the company was not very close to reality.

At the word of the additional sweetener, Darcy started having some serious second thoughts about leaving. "Okay Bob, so far you've been very general. Let's get down to some details. How much more money? What departments will I pick up? And—not that I am hoping for your demise anytime soon—how much is this very large payout?" Bob flashed her a big smile.

At that moment, he knew he had her hooked.

# CALM BEFORE
# THE STORM

**Darcy sat in her office** late one Friday afternoon three months after the conference room meeting that changed her working life forever. As she reflected on that day, she wondered if she had made the right decision. So far, Ron had stayed out of the day-to-day running of her accounting department. But it was quite clear that his influence was still very strong in the administration and warehouse operations that he had overseen as an operations manager. The managers in these departments were weak, and it seemed no one could make a decision without running it up the flagpole to Ron. It wasn't that they were incompetent or didn't know their jobs; they were just plain scared to decide anything for fear of the consequences if they were wrong. Because Ron had to bless every little change, both departments were slow and inefficient. This was compounded by the fact that years of double-digit revenue growth had put a strain on the support departments. The infrastructure of the company was crumbling before her very eyes. Darcy knew to get the results that were necessary she would need to make changes on the management level in both departments as soon as possible.

Darcy's working relationship with Ron had improved since the meeting. She had decided that she would try to engage Ron as much as she could. He had asked for her input, and she was sure going to give it. At first, it seemed to go well. He was open to discussing her concerns, many of which had to do with his old departments. Though she was determined not to allow her authority to be diluted, she decided to inform Ron of any changes she planned to make well in advance of doing so.

She did her best to understand Ron's point of view. She kept reminding herself that they were two very different people who approached things in very different ways. She began to read business books and articles that talked about how different personalities work together. One book gave her great reason to pause.

*The Danger Zone* by Jerry Mills illustrates the three types of personalities in every business: Finders, Minders, and Grinders. The Finders, according to the author, are the leaders in an organization; they spend 80 percent of their time on business development, and are also the visionaries. The Minders are the very important people who *mind* the shop. They are the ones who get into the minutia of the business and make sure things are running properly—they are normally the middle managers who only have Grinders as direct reports. The Grinders are the people who do the actual work of the company, normally wageworkers that are more task oriented, they typically don't need to worry about anything but their task at hand.

While reading the book, it became clear to Darcy that Ron was a textbook Minder, not a Finder. He was certainly more concerned about whether Susie in the warehouse was jumping on the internet during the day, rather than what strategies could be used to break into the elusive upper and middle market companies throughout the state. Because of Ron's Minder ways, all the middle managers that had worked for him over the years had been pushed into Grinder roles. To Darcy, this was a foreshadowing of things to come, as Mills was very clear in the book that having a Minder at the top spot in any company will more than likely lead to stagnation.

Darcy decided to concentrate first on the administration department, as there was a growing level of tension between them and the sales department. Billing issues were causing problems with many customers, and Lisa, the manager, could not seem to get control of the situation. Her consistent response to the many complaints from Sales was that she was understaffed and her team was unable to keep up with the growing customer base.

After observing the department and looking at industry benchmarks for staffing in an admin department for a company their size, it was clear to Darcy that the problem wasn't the fact that they were understaffed, but that the people they had were not working efficiently. When Darcy tried to talk to Lisa about the problems, she sensed that Lisa had long ago stopped taking ownership for her responsibilities, as there was an apparent lack of urgency and caring. It was too bad because Darcy had been involved in the interview process a few years earlier when Lisa was hired. She had come to them with a stellar record of performance managing a department like the one she was now responsible for, but was no longer the young manager with such great potential that Darcy had come to know during their interview.

Darcy began the recruiting process for Lisa's replacement. When she told Ron that she planned to replace Lisa, she sensed a slight annoyance on his part, but he didn't object. After a few weeks of what seemed like non-stop interviewing, Betty finally walked through the door. She and Darcy hit it off immediately. Betty Carson was a middle-aged, no-nonsense Minder, who had a solid background managing young people for success. She thrived on the two things the young staff needed most: mentorship and quality control.

Darcy hired Betty and gave her free rein to make the necessary changes in the department to ensure success. Betty climbed into the trenches and spent several months reviewing procedures, cleaning up contracts that were set up improperly, assessing (hiring and firing) staff, and also mending a very contentious relationship with the Sales department. In fact, Betty quickly became every salesperson's best friend. Months later, the department which had been "understaffed" before Betty's arrival, ended up with one less person due to increased efficiencies and quality control.

While Betty was doing her magic over in the admin department, Darcy started to dive into the mess in the warehouse. Inventory turns (the calculation of how many times inventory turns over per year) had been outrageously bad for years, but every time Darcy had tried to offer her assistance she had always been shut down. This would be an opportunity to make a difference. She knew the warehouse was Ron's baby and she needed to tread lightly so as not to disrupt their much better working relationship. Bad inventory turns had always been a problem for her. She felt that the ongoing cash flow issues in the company were at least in part due to excess inventory and archaic ordering procedures. However, her concerns always seemed to fall on deaf ears. Regarding parts and supplies, Ron would always dismissively respond that he was working on it and it was all under control. Then there was the equipment inventory.

When it came to over-ordering, Bob was the company's biggest culprit. All the major vendors had to do was call Bob and offer a volume discount. Always the dealmaker, he would buy hundreds of thousands of dollars in unneeded equipment. Unfortunately, even though he was in retirement, the one way he made sure he remained relevant was by continuing to handle the negotiations for equipment buys. This had a huge impact on the sales department, because much of the cash was tied up in equipment inventory that was not selling. It was impossible to stock the equipment that was needed. Therefore, the lag time between a sale and installation was often longer than it should have been.

Darcy recognized that it was futile to try to convince Bob to give up equipment ordering, so she decided she needed to start by assessing the parts and supplies situation. Her first observation was that most of the ordering was being done outside of the rather robust enterprise resource planning (ERP) software that had been implemented a few years earlier. Instead of trusting what the software was telling the parts and supplies clerks to order, they were trusting their instincts, as well as allowing the technicians who serviced the machines in the field to decide what they would and would not carry in their car stocks.

It became obvious to Darcy that this way of ordering was not working due to the high volume of inventory write-downs being done quarterly because of obsolescence. Darcy contacted the software company and scheduled classes for the clerks to learn how to auto-stock both the warehouse and the technicians' vehicles based upon usage, and the model and make of every machine in the field. This is a complex calculation that no one could ever do accurately in their head.

When Darcy told the warehouse manager, Clint, what she had done, his first response was, "Are you sure this is okay with Ron?" Darcy tried her best to not show her annoyance. Clint was another manager who, instead of identifying a problem and fixing it, was waiting for Ron to swoop in and save the day. Knowing Ron as she did, Darcy was sure that's exactly what he wanted from his warehouse guy.

During the process of getting the inventory clerks trained it became evident that Shelly, the parts clerk who had been with the company for about ten years, was not on board with her new procedures. She especially liked the control she had when it came to filling parts orders for the technicians. There were constant complaints about orders not being filled in their entirety, or not being filled in a timely manner for a customer whose machine was completely down. Darcy encouraged Clint to act swiftly on the problem before a lot of good training went to waste.

Clint's response was, "Oh, that's just Shelly. Darcy, she's been here forever. Shelly's going to do what Shelly wants to do." At that, Darcy left Clint's office and headed to the human resources department to see how long it would take to "career adjust" both Clint and Shelly. Fortunately, Shelly had been written up several times for insubordination, which shocked Darcy. That situation was remedied by the end of the day.

With Clint it was a different story. It was the same problem she had run into with Lisa in the admin department. Apparently, Ron, for whatever reason, did not do annual reviews on his direct reports. So, neither manager had any documentation in the file. With Lisa, the solution was easy. Darcy was able to offer her a non-management position in the admin department, which had been met with sheer joy from Lisa, who was tired and burned out as a manager. Clint, on the other hand, would not go so easily. He was Ron's guy. Darcy decided that first thing in the morning she would contact Ron, who was out of town, and talk to him about the Clint situation.

The next morning while on her way to the office, Darcy received a call on her cell phone. The ID showed that it was Ron—he never called unless it was something bad. Her guess was that Clint had something to do with it. She answered in her best smiling voice, "Hey, Ron. How's Tampa? Much warmer than here, I'm sure."

Ron's agitated voice came over the phone, "Darcy, what's going on in the warehouse? Clint called me last night. He was very upset. He said you're coming in and making all kinds of changes. Why was I not told about all of this?"

"Well, Ron, you're out of town, and I felt we needed to go ahead and take care of this Shelly situation given the fact that she should have been fired a long time ago," Darcy said. "I was planning to call you this morning because I'm also increasingly concerned that Clint is another person that needs to go soon. He refused to take ownership of the fact that he had an employee who was disruptive and routinely insubordinate. Shelly was causing a real morale problem that he was totally ignoring. The only problem is that there is nothing good or bad in his file because apparently he's never had a performance appraisal."

There was a long silence. Finally, Ron blurted out, "Darcy, don't do anything else until I get back in town and we've had a chance to talk about this."

"Listen, Ron, I don't plan on firing Clint today, but I have inquired about what documentation we'll need. You said you would stay out of my way. I have tried my best to keep you in the loop as much as possible, but I'm not going to stop progress if you aren't available," Darcy said as she pulled into her parking space. "We'll talk when you get back next week, but I don't think I'm going to change my opinion of Clint. Safe travels, Ron." With that, she heard a mumbled goodbye on the other end, and she hung up. *It's going to be another great day*, she thought.

When the next Monday arrived, Darcy decided to get the discussion with Ron out of the way early. She had been dreading the confrontation since their call the previous week. As Darcy approached Ron's office, she could tell he was annoyed with her for not waiting on him to summon her.

"Hi Ron," she said trying her best to sound friendly. "How was your trip?"

Ron looked up at her and said, "Have a seat. The trip was good until I got the call from Clint. What the hell were you thinking, firing Shelly like that? You know she's well-liked around here. I'm sure many of our employees are wondering what's going on."

"To tell you the truth, Ron, I've had several people tell me how happy they are I made the change. Shelly was the source of a lot of morale issues in both the warehouse and the service department," Darcy said, trying to remain calm. "I don't make it a habit of keeping bad employees just because I like them. Besides, her employee file gave me plenty of reason to make the decision I made. As I said to you earlier, Clint should have fired her a long time ago. While we are on the subject, it's my opinion that Clint is a very weak manager, and though he knows the business well, he should never have been promoted to a position where he supervises people."

Darcy could see a flash of anger come over Ron's face. "Darcy, I'm telling you right now: do not make any more personnel decisions without talking to me first. As far as I'm concerned, the Clint discussion is off the table right now."

Darcy stood up as she said, "Well, I guess this conversation is over. Have a great day."

As she walked back to her office, Darcy seriously considered calling Bob. Her conversations with him had become much less frequent, and she feared that Ron was becoming Bob's only line of communication to the company. Not knowing how he would react to a call complaining about Ron, she decided to suck it up and just try to move forward. Besides, the business opportunity that she was ready to leave for months earlier was no longer available. That door had closed and she was feeling trapped. It was as if the walls were closing in on her.

During Darcy's several months of observing the warehouse operations, another, much bigger problem came to light. She had always heard a lot of complaints from the sales department about how long it took to have the product delivered to a customer after the sales paperwork was signed. The ordering and receiving delays due to the inventory issues were only part of the problem. There was a real logistical nightmare in how a new machine moved through the ordering, receiving, set-up, and delivery processes. There wasn't a standard means of communication between the warehouse and sales departments on when something was needed and when there was availability for delivery.

Darcy could see countless examples of over-promising and under-delivering to the customer. It was obvious that there needed to be some mediation and procedure literature for both Sales and the warehouse. Darcy decided to put together a committee that included a representative from every area of the business affected by the "order to delivery" process. She asked Pete Haines, one of the regional sales managers; Julie Tillman, the warehouse logistics person; John Norris from the service department; and Beth Little from Admin to serve on the committee. In addition, she brought in Trisha Marshall, the corporate trainer and procedure writer.

At first, the meetings contained a lot of finger pointing. She was quickly seeing a common theme: no one wanted to take ownership of anything. Trisha then decided to use the whiteboard to try to come up with a visual on what the process should look like in order to determine at what points in the process they were experiencing delays. Of course, they only attacked the problems they could fix. Expanding inventory was off the table due to tight cash flow, but they did come up with a way to get inventory ordered faster, which reduced "order to delivery" by at least one day. Another problem was incomplete sales paperwork—many in Sales did whatever they could to skirt the system. Quite often paperwork was being kicked back, which could add days to the process. Pete completely agreed that the sales department was part of the problem and seemed to really want to fix it. Now they were getting somewhere.

The service department complained that they weren't getting enough information to plan for installation. It took time to call the customer to get what they needed. Logistics chimed in that they were constantly running into problems for the delivery guys, such as failure to mention that there were stairs and other tricky issues that would require more than one person to complete the delivery. Subsequent re-schedules added days to the process, but it also made the company look bad in the eyes of the customer.

All agreed there should be changes to the information required from the sales department, which must be completed before it could be turned in. Pete felt that it would be well-received by most in the sales department, but he did warn that there would be push back from some of the most senior reps. Darcy made sure she kept Ron informed about everything they were doing. She thought she was doing all she could to avoid another blow-up.

# AMBUSH

**Darcy's committee spent several** weeks putting together a very comprehensive plan along with the revised paperwork. Everyone agreed that the exercise had not only produced a great end product, but the process they had gone through to get there was stimulating. The departments at Burgess Industries typically worked in silos, and it became clear to everyone that it was much easier to fix a problem when everyone worked toward the same goal.

The next step was to set up a meeting with the entire sales department to roll out the new procedures and present the new paperwork requirements. Darcy was uncertain how that would turn out, given Pete's prior warnings that there might be some pushback. But they felt that by first presenting the number of days they had knocked off "order to delivery" would make things more palatable.

Over the next few days prior to the sales meeting, it became obvious to Darcy that some in the sales department had already heard about the changes. Not that they were working in secret, but she had hoped her committee would have waited for the formal roll-out of the process before talking about it so it could be presented properly. Some of the off-hand comments she heard made it obvious to her that Pete had been correct in his prediction: she might have a bit of a fight on her hands.

On the day of the meeting, Darcy was happy to see practically everyone in the sales department in attendance, along with some people from Service and Admin as well. The committee sat at the front of the training room and waited until everyone was seated. At the last minute, Ron walked in with Elaine Johnson, the manager of the major account sales representatives.

As Darcy began, Ron spoke up, "Darcy, Elaine and I have been talking, and there are some valid objections to the amount of customer information you want to require the salespeople to obtain. They simply don't have the time to do that." Darcy was flabbergasted. She had been over all of this with Ron. It became obvious to her that it wasn't her committee that had leaked the information. It had been Ron.

Why in the world would he not have brought up these objections in private? Instead, here she was in front of half of the company being completely undermined. Trying to stay calm, Darcy started, "Ron, everything looked fine to you just the other day. Why are you just now bringing up these objections? This committee was made up of representatives from each stakeholder department. We all agreed that this process would cut four to five days from 'order to delivery.' This has been an issue for a long time."

"Well Darcy, I guess you should have included Elaine and me in those meetings, so you could get a more realistic idea of what would work and not work. Don't get me wrong, I don't hate all of it. Your new process for ordering is great. It's just this new paperwork is way too cumbersome."

Darcy knew the longer she stood there and tried to argue with Ron the more foolish she would look. There had to be an agenda behind his actions. It was clear from the looks she was getting that everyone in that room recognized it too. She quickly adjourned the meeting and apologized for inconveniencing everyone.

Once she collected herself, Darcy went to Ron to find out what happened since they last talked. He had seemed totally on board. She also wanted to find out why he humiliated her in front of all those people.

When she reached his office, he quickly gestured her to come in and sit down. "Listen, Darcy, I know what you are going to say. I felt I had to handle this appropriately because the rumor mill was running rampant."

Darcy paused a few seconds, "Well whose fault is that? If you have been talking to Elaine about it, then you know everyone in the sales department has heard about it. Ron, the truth is you blindsided me and everyone in that room knew it. The only question is why you would do that to a colleague?"

"Oh, Darcy. Stop being so dramatic. I'm sorry. I didn't mean to embarrass you. By the way, while you're here, I want to talk to you about something else. You know when I took this job it left a hole in operations. Ted Davis has expressed an interest in becoming our new Chief Operating Officer. He's very good with numbers and cares deeply about saving money for the company. I've decided to promote him and put him over the warehouse operation."

Darcy stared at him for what seemed like an eternity. She was shocked, but when she thought about it, it made a lot of sense. Ron was not happy with what she was doing in his warehouse. Ted was a great guy, but he had been in sales his whole career and, by her count, had only supervised one person in the twenty years he had been with the company. His appeal to Ron was that he likely wouldn't make even the smallest of moves in the warehouse without having Ron right there to advise him.

"Well this came out of right field, Ron. I'm sure you've already talked to Bob, and he's probably expecting my call. That debacle we all just witnessed with the Sales department gave you some ammunition against me, right?"

"Come on Darcy," Ron started, "you're doing a great job in Admin. Betty has really turned things around. This will give you more time to concentrate on making it even better. Also, you and Ted seem to get along well. I'm sure he'd be open to suggestions on how to get the inventory situation under control. Yes, I have talked to Bob, and he thinks it's a good idea. Everyone in the warehouse likes Ted. It will be a good fit."

This time leaving Ron's office, she again wondered whether it was even worth calling Bob. She decided she couldn't let this happen without at least expressing her opposition.

When she finally reached Bob later that afternoon, her frustration was almost too much to bear. "Hi, Bob. I hope you and Jill are enjoying your retirement. Please give her my best. I'm sure you were expecting my call, so I'll get right to the point. Please tell me how Ron sold this COO change to you, and why wasn't I involved in any discussions?"

"Well Darcy, he said that overseeing three departments was becoming too much for you, and that he wanted you to concentrate more on the Admin area and its transformation. I thought his proposal to promote Ted was a good one. Everyone loves Ted, and he's been a loyal employee for many years. I was under the impression that you and Ron had talked about it and that you were on board."

"How in the world did you get that impression?" she asked. "He just informed me of it right after totally undermining me in a sales meeting. I just don't know what to say right now."

"Darcy, you know that our communication around here has always sucked," he said with a laugh. "I blame myself for that. However, we can't un-promote Ted. I am really sorry you had to hear about it this way, though." Darcy could feel those "golden handcuffs"—the things like good pay and benefits given to key employees to entice them to remain with the company—getting tighter and tighter.

"Bob, you always use the 'communication' excuse when something like this happens. The way I see it is you and Ron are the only ones with that problem. Why haven't you ever done anything to fix it?"

"Well, I guess Ron and I are alike in that we just put our heads down and try to get the job done without thinking about who we need to talk to," he said. "Again, I'm sorry, and I will certainly talk to Ron about doing a better job at keeping you in the loop."

Darcy truly believed that Bob was sincere about the way he worked, but she couldn't help but think that Ron's lack of communication was a little more agenda driven. Unfortunately, she was never going to convince Bob of that. She realized that she was wasting her time trying to talk about this. Her best course of action was to just move forward, and try her best to work with Ted to at least fix some of the inventory problems.

"Darcy, before you go, I'd like to talk to you about a phone call that I got the other day. It brings up another good reason to free up some of your time. You see, there is this group of investors that is targeting dealerships throughout the East Coast. They want to buy a group of ten to twenty different dealerships to take advantage of all the good things that come with size. They are looking at us to possibly be one of their anchor dealerships. They'd like to come in and meet with us next week. Ron isn't going to be happy, but it never hurts to test the waters."

This piqued Darcy's interest. Perhaps throwing herself into this project would give her time to lick her wounds after everything that had happened that day. She was excited about the upcoming meeting with the Sterling Group. Her thoughts went back to Bob's statements about how he would "take care" of her and Ron if he ever sold the company. Still not knowing what that meant, it certainly brought up thoughts of a way out of an increasingly untenable working environment.

Over the next few days, she had several conversations with Ted regarding the parts and supplies inventories. Ted's promotion was announced with little fanfare, but Darcy couldn't avoid the fact that people were treating her a little differently; she was damaged goods. She enjoyed working with Ted, but it was obvious that improvements in the warehouse were going to continue to move at a snail's pace. Ted had some great ideas on how to save the company money, but, if they didn't conform to the way Ron wanted things to run, they were shot down before any discussion.

And although Clint had fought her on the additional training for the two clerks, she had managed to pull rank and get that done while she was still in charge of the department. Now there would be no excuses for the crazy purchasing procedures. Darcy and Ted decided it might be a good idea to try to somehow incentivize the two clerks for improvements in the inventory turns and obsolescence numbers. Darcy was sure to map it out as clearly as possible so Ted could present it to Ron since he would be the one to make or break their idea.

Fortunately, Ron was open to the idea since he was desperate for Ted to have success in the department. The two of them set up a meeting with the two warehouse clerks to discuss how they could make a difference for the company, in addition to making a few extra dollars.

Darcy was surprised at the level of skepticism with which they were met. Neither clerk believed they had the level of control to make a difference in inventory levels, expressing their thoughts on how there were too many buying decisions being made outside of the department, and that their efforts would constantly be undermined. They were happy about the effort that Darcy and Ted were making, but neither had illusions that they would be seeing any extra money anytime soon.

Sure enough, two days later, one of the major vendors called Bob about a quarter-end inventory buy. Bob, always the negotiator, knew that there wasn't a short-term need for the equipment they were trying to sell him, so he got them to throw in what turned out to be about nine months' inventory of supplies at special pricing. From Bob's perspective, he was saving the company a ton of money. From Darcy, Ted, and the supplies clerks' perspectives, the whole incentive plan that they had spent hours putting together was now completely undercut. Darcy couldn't help but wonder how much of those supplies would eventually end up on an obsolescence list.

## A WAY OUT?

**John Sterling was a flashy sales guy** who had been involved with many acquisitions in the industry on both sides during the 1980s and 90s when there was a lot of mergers and acquisitions (M&A) activity with the major vendors. Bob had been approached by potential buyers on a couple of occasions in the past twelve years, so Darcy was already aware of how the process worked. They made it all the way to a letter of intent (LOI) and due diligence one time several years earlier, only to have Bob get cold feet as they approached a final offer.

Darcy found the whole process exhilarating. She remembered Ron had almost worried himself to death. The last thing he had wanted then was for Bob to sell the company. Obviously, he was going to be even more opposed this time, because right now he had total control of things as president. Darcy really couldn't blame him.

No doubt, his life would change dramatically if Bob ever sold and he would become accountable to someone.

The meeting with John started with the three of them outlining the strengths of the company and any plans for future growth. She had to admit: Ron was great in meetings like this. He was very good at communicating the company story. Where he got a little fuzzy was in communicating a vision, Bob jumped in and saved the conversation. Darcy's role was to tell the story of the solid financial growth they had experienced for the past decade.

Afterward, John met with each of them privately to get their individual impressions of the company. Darcy did her best to talk about all that was good about this company that she dearly loved. But one question that John asked made her pause for a few seconds. He asked Darcy to tell him what kind of leader Ron was. When she didn't answer immediately, he tried to clarify.

"Is he controlling, or does he give his managers some leeway?"

Darcy chose her words carefully. "Well, I think he definitely leans more toward controlling."

"Interesting," said John. "I picked up on that in our meeting earlier. No worries, though. I still think this would be a good fit for us. Are you ready to dig into the numbers?"

"Absolutely," said Darcy.

Over the next few weeks, Darcy was introduced to Steve Chase, the CFO of the Sterling Group. He sent a list of items Darcy needed to compile so they could come up with a baseline valuation prior to due diligence. They were trying to come up with an estimate to see if they were anywhere close to Bob's number. Darcy did her best to identify all the owner addbacks (expenses that would go away once Bob was no longer there), plus any non-recurring, extraordinary expenses that may be depressing their EBITDA (earnings before interest, taxes, depreciation, and amortization). A multiple of this number was usually the basis for a valuation in the industry. Steve and Darcy quickly built a great working relationship. They talked by phone almost daily, and Darcy felt that Steve was very sincere in his goal to come up with a fair offer. Darcy was working day and night to make this a successful transaction, because she really thought it was what Bob wanted.

Finally, she received a call from Bob a few days after her final update for Steve. She felt very good that she had uncovered everything that could be useful to the Sterling Group, giving the best picture of the financial state of Burgess Industries. She was, quite literally, worn out.

"Hey Darcy," said Bob in his booming voice. "I wanted to let you know that I finally received an offer from Sterling."

"Really? I kind of thought we were close," she said. "Steve and I have been working day and night to get this thing done."

"Wonderful," Bob said. "I can't tell you how much I appreciate all of your efforts."

"So, when am I going to get a look at the LOI?" she asked, hardly able to contain her anticipation. Would this finally be her ticket to freedom?

"Of course, I'll send it over this afternoon," he said. "I'll be in the office tomorrow afternoon, and we can discuss."

"Very good. I'll talk to you then, Bob."

Darcy waited the entire afternoon for a copy of the LOI. Bob had not disclosed anything about it in their conversation, so reading it for the first time would tell her everything. He had not even acknowledged whether or not he felt it was fair, or if it was just another waste of her time. She knew that she was the only one who had anything invested in this deal so far.

She finally received the document, and when reading through found everything to look straightforward. When she got to the sales price, she was happy to see that it was very close to the number that Bob said he needed to make this thing happen. As she reached the last paragraph in the agreement, her jaw dropped open in shock as she read, "John Sterling, Steve Chase, Bob Burgess, and Ron Marchetti, as officers of the company, will hold equity positions in the percentages as stated below. Employment contracts for a period of five years will be required of Ron Marchetti and Darcy Holtzman, recognizing their importance to the on-going operations of the company."

Darcy couldn't believe what she was reading. Was this what Bob meant when he said he was going to take care of her? A contract with no equity, no bonus, and with the only guarantee being that she would be working for Ron for another five years. The thought of that was excruciating. She thought back on the years of dedication she had put into the company, and the many opportunities she had passed up because she believed that she was more than just another employee. Bob always made her believe that she was part of the reason Burgess was such a successful company.

The next day when Bob popped his head in her doorway and asked, "So what did you think?" She answered, "Well, Bob, it looks like a good deal for you. Ron also comes out looking good. However, I see one problem: there is no way I'm going to sign an employment contract. There is absolutely no advantage in that for me. Bob, I've been working day and night trying to help you put this deal together because I thought it was what you wanted, while Ron has done nothing to advance the effort. Yet, he comes out of this with an equity stake, and I must sign away the next five years of my life with no equity or compensation guarantees. I'm sorry but I expected more than that given my contribution to the success of this company.

Bob looked at her sheepishly and said, "Darcy, you know that Ron is all out opposed to this deal. We were afraid that he was going to do something to screw it up, so John thought this would appease him."

By now she saw red. "Are you telling me that I have been working my ass off to help you make this deal work, and Ron is the one who is benefiting because he's not cooperative? I certainly hope this deal doesn't hinge on me signing a contract, because I will not."

"Darcy, what do you expect me to do?" he asked. "I'm just taking their advice on what I need to do to close the deal."

"Bob, did you ever stop and think about how I would react to this? This is a common pattern on how things are done around here. I'll be honest: I'm sick of it. Listen, Bob, I'll do whatever I can to help you make this happen. But I'm sorry, I won't sign an employment agreement."

The next few weeks as they started the due diligence, it seemed that a lot of the momentum for the deal was starting to wane. Bob, once again, became disengaged, and it was almost comical how Ron suddenly became the go-to guy for Sterling's due diligence team. Darcy had lost all interest, but went through the motions when asked for the continual updates to her previous numbers.

As hard as she tried, she could not mask the hurt she felt at what Bob had done. It told her that he had no intention of "taking care" of her when he finally did decide to sell. What hurt the most is that when he had convinced her to stay months earlier it was partially under false pretenses. One thing she was certain of going forward was that her relationship with Bob would never quite be the same.

As the due diligence continued and the Sterling people started looking at the internal workings of the company, they noted several areas of concern in a memorandum to Bob:

1. Though it is good to see that operations are not overly dependent on Bob Burgess, it is clear after interviewing the department heads that there is a great reluctance on the

part of managers to do anything without an okay by Ron Marchetti. The over-reliance on one person—in this case, Ron—is problematic.

2.  After years of averaging double-digit growth, the current year interim financial statements are showing sales have stagnated, and profits are down from the same time last year.

3.  Very little time seems to have been spent recently on strategic planning for future sales growth. Day-to-day operations seem to consume the time of the people who should be taking on a visionary role. No time has been spent on forecasting and budgeting.

4.  An over-reliance on revenue from low-profit deals and low-profit contracts has led to a severe cash flow problem that will not be able to be fixed in the short term.

5.  We see no real efforts to differentiate Burgess from their closest competitors. Again, no effective strategic marketing plan is in place.

6.  Darcy Holtzman's inability to commit in writing to the ongoing success of the business is problematic.

Based on the concerns that Sterling found, they came back to Bob with a revised offer reduced by about one-third. For Bob that was a non-starter. After dozens of weekends and late night hours compiling information, Darcy knew, once again, it was all a waste of time. Just as before, the deal stagnated, but this time it was not a harmless exercise. This time, it had caused irreparable damage. Darcy now had to decide what her future would be with Burgess. Given the salary and perks, another offer would need to be lucrative. Though she knew it would probably be a useless effort, she vowed to herself to start testing the job market.

# A NEW DIRECTION

**During his first year as president**, everyone started to notice just how many business trips Ron was taking. Every vendor meeting or trade organization meeting available to go to, Ron was there. It seemed he was gone at least one week out of every month.

The business owners that Ron mingled with at these meetings liked him because he volunteered to serve on most of the committees, and even got himself appointed to run some of the events they sponsored. These were tasks the other owners had long since become tired of. Ron also stroked their egos by constantly asking for ideas on how to run a successful dealership.

The managers at Burgess always dreaded Ron's return from these meetings, because he came back with multiple ideas on how he would make the company better. It made sense since Ron wasn't exactly known for his original thinking. However, it was annoying that he continually went outside of the company to come up with ways to improve things. It was as if he had no trust or faith in the group of managers he had assembled to run his various departments. Ron was in search of a magic bullet to help him make the company great. The problem was that many of the ideas he brought back were either non-scalable, or weren't right for the market that Burgess Industries served. When the initiatives failed, the blame fell on the managers for not supporting Ron's "great ideas."

After one such dealer meeting, Ron came back with a mission much larger than anything he had previously undertaken. The industry leaders had decided that a natural progression would be to start including IT services as part of their offerings. This made a lot of sense because, in recent years, the salespeople were talking less to regular purchasing agents and more to the IT directors.

The office products business had evolved over the years; first with stand-alone analogue machines, then to multi-function devices that were connected to servers and that could print, scan, fax, as well as copy. The industry was now technology based. Ron was convinced that they needed to jump into the IT arena immediately or Burgess would be left behind the curve.

Within a few months, he and the in-house IT director, Amy Cho, had bought software and hired a new technician. Voila, they had a new division called Burgess Managed IT. This had all been done with virtually no communication with the other departments in the company. No forecast, no budget, no plans for on-boarding new customers, and no direction to the Sales department.

The software was a project-based system that integrated with a basic accounting package. This entire system was set up to run outside the ERP (the company's operating software) that Burgess ran for the office products division. Amy set up the whole system with no input from the accounting department. The result worked for the IT people, but the accounting side was a mess. By the time Darcy's group was engaged to maintain the system, the changes that needed to be made were both difficult and time-consuming. Useful reporting was virtually non-existent. They eventually started producing financials for the division in an Excel spreadsheet. After six months, and tens of thousands of dollars, Amy had brought on only a couple of customers to whom she had promised the world to secure the business.

Ron used his dealer contacts to get a membership for them in an IT services trade organization. He and Amy travelled quarterly to meetings where they shared numbers and discussed techniques on how to improve the business. It was hard to tell who was running the department because Ron was making all the decisions and driving all the discussions on why things didn't seem to be turning around.

Meanwhile, Amy and her technician were being run ragged by the few customers they had. The contracts they were writing promised way too much on-site time; Amy had no time to manage anything. She constantly begged for help, but the revenue they were producing was not coming close to covering the cost to run the department. Bringing on more people would send the department even further into the red.

Darcy and the other department heads wondered how the decision had been made to grow the new division organically. No one had been asked their opinion on how they should proceed. Since the IT arena was completely outside of their wheelhouse, most felt it would have been better to buy a small but well-run IT services company already equipped with the basic infrastructure necessary to become a productive arm of the business. At the very least, they should have hired a manager who had experience in growing a similar company. Amy was smart and good at running an in-house IT department, but she had no experience doing what she was being asked to do.

The division plugged along, and the losses grew from tens of thousands to hundreds of thousands of dollars. Eventually, Ron decided that the reason the division was not growing was due to Amy's incompetence. In perfect Ron form, instead of firing her, he began to make her life miserable by denigrating her at every turn. Within a few months, Amy quit, and the new division was on life support.

# DARYL THE DISRUPTOR

**While Ron waited for Amy to quit,** he started getting the wheels in motion to fix the IT services department and the less-than-impressive sales numbers—both at the same time. For quite a while, he had been in secret negotiations to bring over one of the heavy hitters, Daryl Hughes, from the sales division of their largest competitor to run Burgess's sales department. Daryl had a few years' experience running an IT services operation, and Ron thought he was being clever by poaching a competitor's employee because he knew there would be a non-compete agreement of at least a year that would have to be dealt with. The solution would be to bring Daryl in and give him a year to get the IT services division on its feet.

Meanwhile, he could learn about Burgess's sales operation at arm's length while he worked through his non-compete agreement. After a year, he would take over the entire sales operation.

Almost as soon as Amy quit, Daryl was hired, and Ron assembled his team to explain what Daryl would be doing. The first question was whether Daryl would be working directly with the customers as Amy had. Ron's answer was no. They would need another technician to handle customer visits. Darcy couldn't help but envision dollar signs flying out the window. The division would now be paying for another high-dollar technician, plus Daryl's rather substantial salary for a year.

She hoped that Daryl would be able to turn this thing around quickly, because the losses since the division started were closing in on the one-million-dollar mark. She was beginning to believe that they would never start making money in IT Services. Her only hope was that it would one day become cash flow positive. It had been a terrible drain on an already dire cash situation. That's why she was surprised that Bob had let it go on long as he had.

Though she and Bob hardly ever talked anymore, she knew he received her monthly financial statements, which highlighted how poorly the IT services division was doing. He had to know what damage was being done to the value of his company. Darcy guessed that Bob was being given a rosier picture of how things were progressing. But since Ron was the only person in the company with whom he spoke, Bob was easily duped.

To add insult to injury, as the on-boarding process started for Daryl, his previous employer chose to go after Burgess due to Daryl's non-compete agreement. Burgess's attorneys were very good, and defended the company's position well. However, those good attorneys were also expensive. The attorney fees over the next few months came close to thirty thousand dollars. All Darcy could think was, *This guy had better be worth it.*

Daryl was the first upper-level manager who had been hired from the outside in several years. Certainly, the only one since Ron had taken over. He came in wanting to make a difference quickly. The "Burgess Way" was completely foreign to him.

Soon, he began to run into some of the same roadblocks that Darcy experienced when she was trying to turn around her two departments. His frustration could be seen daily. The other managers thought that he had a lot of good ideas, but Ron undermined everything he tried to implement.

Late one evening as she was preparing to leave, Darcy could hear a heated conversation coming through the thin walls between her office and Ron's.

"Ron, I just don't understand why you even hired me if you aren't going to let me do my job," yelled Daryl.

"Oh, come on Daryl, I'm letting you do your job. I just need you to slow down a bit. The people around here aren't ready for this much change," said Ron.

"Are you kidding me? Everyone around here would welcome change! That is, everyone except you! If you want this company to grow, Ron, you are going to have to let go a little and start trusting your managers." There was a pause.

Then, with much irritation in his voice Ron said, "Daryl, the only reason I make all of the decisions around here is because I'm the only one who ever has any good ideas."

That brought a smile to Darcy's face. The guy was completely clueless. She then heard Ron's office door slam, and Daryl stormed past her without saying a word.

Though their situations were similar, Daryl and Darcy chose to handle things differently. Darcy had lost her fight, and chose to spend her days going through the motions. The failed acquisition had affected her greatly, and she no longer had the energy to attempt to make a difference. The money she was making and lack of opportunities were forcing her to stay. Daryl, on the other hand, decided not to idly sit by and allow his career to be high-jacked by someone who knew nothing about what he was doing.

Daryl began to fight Ron at every turn. Ron was beginning to wonder if he had made the right decision in hiring Daryl. Yet, after spending a lot of money to get him on board, he knew it would look terrible if he got rid of Daryl so quickly.

For the next year, Daryl spent his time attempting to standardize the contracts they were writing for IT Services. The only way to make money was to streamline their offering and make sure that the on-site work they did was minimal. He realized that there were customers that needed to be either renegotiated or fired. Ron fought him passionately on that front. The thought of firing a customer, even a bad one, was foreign to Ron.

Eventually, the department began to stabilize. Though they were still losing money, the direction seemed to be slowly changing. They were three years into the venture and still only had a handful of clients, and they needed several more before they would eventually break even. There had been no analysis of the competition in their home market prior to jumping in. It turned out that you couldn't swing a dead cat in the Charlotte area without hitting an IT services provider. Establishing themselves as a player had become much more difficult than anyone at Burgess could have imagined.

After the expiration of Daryl's non-compete contract, his attention began to be divided between the IT services division and the sales department. He was anxious to get back to the work he loved. The only problem was, once again, there was a huge roadblock standing in the way of getting anything done: Ron.

The first thing Daryl wanted to tackle was the inequity of sales quotas and the commission plans. This had been a common theme from most of the sales reps when he had met with each in the weeks leading up to his takeover of the department. He first called a meeting of all the regional sales managers to get an idea of how the commission plans were derived and how much input each of them had given. In attendance were Ralph Winston, eastern sales manager based in Raleigh; Troy Gordan, northern sales manager based in Greensboro; Pete Haines, western sales manager based in the home office in Charlotte; and Elaine Johnson, major account manager also based in Charlotte. Daryl asked Darcy to join them in case there were any financial questions.

Commissions were a particularly sore subject for the managers who had reps outside of the larger metropolitan areas, because commissions worked under the same quota system even though they were serving a much smaller business population. Daryl began by asking them, "How are quotas set and how are commissions determined?"

Ralph gave a laugh as he answered, "Well, Daryl, your guess is as good as mine. Ron handles writing the commission plans and awarding territories. We have never had any input on any of it. I have some reps based in the Raleigh/Cary area who can make the yearly president's trip without lifting a finger, just because of the renewal business they control. Then I have guys who handle Fayetteville and over toward the beach that work their butts off and are barely able to eke out a living, much less get awarded the trip. It's terribly inequitable. That's why we have such a high turnover rate. But to hear Ron talk, it's because all of us suck as managers."

Troy decided to chime in, "I have the same problem, Daryl. My two top reps in Greensboro may work forty hours a week combined, and make a great living. If I had a couple of hungry people willing to work, I could double the sales in my region in no time. I've mentioned it to Ron, but those two reps are his golden children, and he's afraid we will lose them if we change their commission plans. They have Ron wrapped around their little fingers, and they know it."

Daryl had assumed that there would be some work to do to fix their broken compensation system, but he had no idea that Ron had total control. He then turned to Darcy and asked, "Does your department have any input? It's been my experience that Accounting does a 'sanity check' on plans before they are implemented."

Darcy shook her head and said, "We have no access to the plans. Payroll is just given a summary sheet of what to pay every two weeks. That's the level of our involvement." This really would be a fight. "Okay, let me work on this, and I'll get back to you guys," said Daryl.

"With all due respect, Daryl," said Ralph, "we aren't going to hold our breath."

"Understood," said Daryl. "Why don't we move on? Besides compensation, I need to know what your biggest pain points are in regard to your job and your reps' jobs."

At this point, Elaine jumped in. She had been uncharacteristically quiet so far because her reps were the ones who most benefited from the current compensation plan.

"Daryl, as you know, my reps are in front of buyers for the leading companies in North Carolina daily. We are not only up against all the top dealers in the state, but the manufacturers constantly undercut us with crazy pricing. All my reps have years of experience and know how to negotiate. The problem is, they have no authority to do it. Every negotiation must go through Ron. We are losing deals left and right because we are sitting in front of potential customers and having to say, 'I'll get back to you.' Ron is so far in the weeds trying to do everything, most of the time it takes days for him to respond. If we could get just a little wiggle room, I have no doubt we could close much more business. Why Ron believes that we are going to give away the store is beyond me. That's the only explanation I can think of for his need to personally approve everything."

As Elaine talked, Daryl's head dropped lower and lower in frustration. He was beginning to feel like he was running in quicksand. "Okay, Elaine," said Daryl, "I'll add this to my list of items to discuss with Ron. What's next? Pete, do you have anything?"

Pete Haines was the oldest and most experienced sales manager at Burgess. In fact, Pete could retire at any time and live comfortably on the money he had made working in sales organizations much larger than Burgess. But Pete's passion was in teaching young sales reps how to be successful. He had found his niche at Burgess as the manager for all the newer reps who needed more one on one attention.

"Well, Daryl," Pete started in his slow drawl, "there is one thing that I need to mention. You'll remember when Ron brought in Betsy Norman, that sales trainer he met at the dealers' conference last year. She was adamant that one day out of every week we need to be in the office on the phones all day scheduling appointments. You'll recall that Ron made a decree that everyone in the Sales department keeps that day as a calling day. I'm on board, and it takes a very special exception for anyone on my staff to get out of it. The problem is: I am hearing some grumbling from my guys that not everyone is being held to the same schedule."

Elaine could see everyone's gaze move toward her.

"Okay, okay, I'll admit it," she said. "I told my reps that they didn't have to do it. Ron was okay with it. Let's face it, Pete, my group is different and gets much less value from an exercise like that than yours. I felt it was a waste of time."

"Be that as it may, Elaine," said Pete, "you and Ron made that decision, and it was not communicated to the rest of us. So, to my reps, the exercise looks optional. They are accusing me of being a hard-ass for being so unbending on it." Pete then looked at Daryl, and half smiled. "I guess what I am complaining about is communication around here sucks."

Daryl spent the next few days trying to figure out how to convince Ron that he needed to back off from the sales department, and to give him and the managers some authority to fix the problems. Not an easy conversation, since Ron was the cause of all the problems. Judging by the resistance he got on everything in the IT department he was unsure if he had any hope of succeeding.

Ron was out of town at yet another conference, so Daryl decided to get it out of the way as soon as he returned. On Monday morning, he and Darcy asked Ron for some time to go over a few sales-related matters. At first, Ron was cordial, asking how Daryl was enjoying being back on the sales side of the business.

After a few pleasantries Daryl started by saying, "Ron, Darcy and I had a meeting with the managers the other day, and there were a few concerns that came up that I would like to talk to you about."

Ron stared at him for a minute and said, "Daryl, why wouldn't you have included me in that initial meeting with the managers? I have for all intents and purposes been the sales manager for the past year. It would have been a better transition."

Daryl had not even considered including Ron in the meeting, but knowing Ron as he did, was not surprised by his question.

"First of all," Daryl said, "I wanted to get started as soon as possible and you were not available last week. Second, I felt that it would be easier to get to know the group better without you there."

Annoyed, Ron responded, "I guess next time we should discuss when you plan to bring the management team in. So, what are these concerns you want to bring up with me?"

"Well," Daryl started, "there are a lot of complaints about the inequity of the sales compensation plan. The quotas are set too low for some and too high for others. There also doesn't seem to be any logical explanation for the way the territories have been made up. Also, I see that a couple of our managers are being paid on revenues instead of gross profit. I'm not sure why you would ever do that. I was also surprised to hear from Darcy that she's never been consulted on the plans."

Daryl looked up at Ron and Darcy from his notes and saw that Ron's face had turned a few shades of red.

"Well, Daryl, had you asked me about the compensation plan instead of the managers and Darcy you would have gotten the correct story. This plan came to me from one of our dealers in the Independent Dealers' Association. They are a very successful dealer, and Nate Campbell, the owner, says this plan works well for him. As for consulting with Darcy, I see no need." There was a visible look of annoyance on Darcy's face, but she held her tongue. She was here to support Daryl.

Daryl looked slightly puzzled and said, "Ron, I know Nate, and I could see how this plan works for him. His dealership is in a large metropolitan area, and all his sales territories are uniform. Our geographic makeup is completely different. You just can't have the same plan for someone in Raleigh and someone in Lumberton. The managers are admitting to me that they have some rich territories in the larger areas that aren't being worked to their fullest extent because the reps don't have to. They are being paid very good money to just sit around. Meanwhile, we're losing potentially good people in the less populated areas because it's virtually impossible for them to make a living under this plan."

Ron was not convinced. "Listen Daryl, I know you are talking about Chuck and Debra up in Greensboro, and Phil and Lori over in Raleigh. We need to keep those reps—they're our best. If I change their plans, they will leave, and we will be dead in the water."

Daryl tried to stay calm, but it wasn't easy given Ron's total disregard for the big picture. "Ron, I don't see it that way. I think those guys may have once been good reps, but they are now a drag on the company. I could find you people in both of those markets who could eclipse the sales of those four reps in a matter of months."

Ron was beginning to tire of the conversation. "Bottom line is I can't risk it. As for the managers who are paid on revenue, I had to make a couple of one-off exceptions to convince Elaine and Ralph to stay on board. So, I'm not going to change any commission plans right now. What else do you have?"

At that moment Daryl knew that he was wasting his time. He knew that Ron would never give up any of his grasp on anything to do with sales. "I guess the only other thing was that Elaine is concerned that her reps don't have enough negotiating power, and they are losing deals waiting for you to respond to requests for changes. There are also some issues with the fact that policy changes aren't always communicated to everyone."

Ron cocked his head and replied, "Geez, Daryl, sounds like you had yourself a little bitch-session the other day."

Daryl answered, "I just wanted to find out where the pain points are and see if I could help, Ron."

"Well, as for the negotiation of deals, I just don't feel comfortable that any of those guys would be looking out for the company first. I feel more secure if I can see changes before any decisions are made."

"But Ron, Elaine says they are losing deals because they aren't able to act quickly in certain circumstances. They are getting hammered out there. If we can't trust these people, maybe we should get new people."

"Daryl, Elaine tends to exaggerate things a little bit. I suspect things aren't quite as bad as they seem. You come back to me with some proof and we'll talk. Can you elaborate on the communication problem?"

"Sure," said Daryl. "Apparently, you have agreed that the major account reps are no longer required to do calling day. I'm not saying that was a bad decision. It's just that the other Charlotte reps are seeing that and assuming that calling day is optional. Pete is coming off as a tyrant because he is being an enforcer on it."

"Oh yeah," responded Ron. "That was my bad. I totally forgot to tell anyone."

"Ron, that's the kind of thing that can cause a real morale problem in a company," said Daryl.

"Point taken. I'll work on that," said Ron dismissively.

As Daryl and Darcy walked to their offices they gave each other a look of frustration showing they both realized just how much a waste of time the meeting was. Today marked one week on the job as Director of Sales, and Daryl knew he had accomplished nothing.

# A WAY OUT (PART 2)

**One day out of the blue,** Darcy received an email from Bob, which said, "Hey, Darce—Give me a call when you get a chance ... Bob."

That was very strange to Darcy, because it had been months since she and Bob had spoken. There was the occasional email when Bob needed money or had a question on a bill that needed to be paid, but she could not remember the last time they talked on the phone.

When Bob picked up, she could feel a sense of unfamiliarity that had never been there before. There wasn't the banter about how bad their college football team was this year or the questions about each other's children; Bob got right down to business.

"Darcy, I got a call from another group that sounds a lot like Sterling. They want to meet with us in a couple of weeks to talk about a possible acquisition."

Darcy hoped that Bob couldn't sense that she was rolling her eyes at that moment.

"Just tell me what you need me to do," she said. "I will say that you need to be aware that the numbers aren't going to look as favorable as they did the last time we went through this. The lagging sales and the drag from the IT services division have significantly hurt the value of the company."

Bob then spoke as if he had not heard her last statement. "You know the drill. As soon as the non-disclosure agreement is signed and sent back, just update the worksheets you were using to report to Sterling, and that should give them a starting point. Thanks in advance for your help on this."

"No problem," she said as she began to hang up the phone.

"Oh, and Darcy," Bob said quickly. Don't say anything to Ron quite yet."

"Okay," she said, thinking that Ron is the last person she would talk to about this.

Darcy sent the reports off to interested group, Great Ridge Imaging, as soon as she could get everything updated to reflect the past few years—they did not look good.

A few days later, she received a call from Bob.

"Hey Darcy, I wanted you to know that I received a verbal from Great Ridge. It was slightly less than Sterling's second offer."

"Yikes," said Darcy, "I guess that makes it a non-starter."

"Well, not really," he said. "I get the feeling they are testing the waters. They seem very excited to move into our footprint. Acquiring us would be a tremendous strategic advantage for them. That's why I told them I would keep lines of communication open, but they would have to come up significantly on their offer before I would entertain anything. What surprised me is that they didn't tell me to pound sand after saying that."

"Are they still going to visit?" asked Darcy.

"Yeah, that's another surprise," he answered. "They obviously don't think it's a waste of time and money to come and see us."

Darcy decided this time she would not get so caught up in the process as she had in the past. Sure, she would provide accurate and timely information as requested, but she would no longer play a proactive role in moving things along. That would be up to Bob and the guys at Great Ridge. As Darcy prepared for the upcoming meeting, she tried her best to find some of the excitement that used to come with these adventures. To her, it was all a waste of time. She knew that Bob would never get the price he wanted. Compound that with the sabotage that Ron would invariably attempt to rain down on the process, and they were most likely on the road to nowhere.

On the day Great Ridge came to visit, Ron was on one of his rampages in the warehouse. Poor Ted was feeling the brunt of it. Ron's way of getting rid of frustration was to displace it on his current whipping boy, and that happened to be Ted this week. Apparently, Ron had caught one of the inventory clerks chatting at Julie's desk, and they were not on break. Ron summoned Ted to his office and proceeded to give him a half-hour lecture on how to control his people. Ted walked out of the meeting with a dazed look on his face. How did he deserve being yelled at like that for such a small infraction? Darcy knew it had nothing to do with what Ron had witnessed in the warehouse, and everything to do with the meeting they would be a part of later that afternoon.

In perfect Bob form, he rolled into the office about two minutes before their guests showed up, giving them no time to discuss what his expectations were for the meeting. That was fine with Ron. In fact, he had spent the entire time after his meeting with Ted in his office with the door closed.

Darcy didn't give it much thought until Bob popped his head into her office and said, "Hey, Darce, how's it going?" Just as she was getting ready to respond, the receptionist buzzed her phone to let her know that the people from Great Ridge had arrived.

Darcy looked up at Bob and said, "So, do you want to go and get Ron? I'd rather not."

Bob flashed her a smile and said, "Sure, but Darcy, he doesn't bite."

"I don't know," she said, "you might want to check with Ted about that." He stared at her with a puzzled look on his face. She just smiled and walked past him on her way to the receptionist's desk.

For a deal that was all but dead, the Great Ridge people sure did bring in their heavy hitters. The CEO, Andrew Ridge, was a bit arrogant, thought Darcy; which explained a lot about the name of his company. Then there was Paul Dugan, the president. Darcy liked him almost immediately. She tagged him as the brains behind the operation. And last, there was Mary Blunt, the CFO. Darcy wondered the purpose for Mary's attendance, as she couldn't have said more than five words during the whole meeting. In fact, after about fifteen minutes of listening to Andrew bloviate about his successful career as a venture capitalist, it was Paul who took over the meeting and clearly articulated the vision for the company.

It was clear that the acquisition of Burgess had been part of that vision for a long time. The guy had done his homework. The footprint and the product representations that Burgess had to offer made them an essential part of their plan for growth throughout the eastern United States.

Darcy couldn't help but think that it was too bad that these guys didn't show up a few years earlier. There was no doubt in her mind that Burgess would have been a part of Great Ridge Imaging had the timing been right.

Another thing Darcy liked about Paul Dugan was that he totally intimidated Ron. The normally articulate Ron was reduced to a blithering idiot. He couldn't answer the easiest of questions. The difference between Paul Dugan and John Sterling was that, while John was strictly a salesperson, Paul knew the business inside out. He had owned and operated one of the most successful dealerships on the West Coast for many years until he sold to Great Ridge. As soon as the ink was dry, Andrew Ridge had offered Paul an equity position in his company and the title of president.

Even though they were far from bridging the gap between Bob's price and the company's true value, it was clear by the end of the meeting that Great Ridge was not going to give up easily.

In subsequent months, Darcy continued to provide updated information to Mary. While she was sure the conversations were continuing between Bob and Paul, she resigned herself to the fact that if this ever happened, she would probably be well into her retirement—and she was counting down the days until that happened.

# THE SMT . . . OR IS IT THE SLT?

**The meeting with Great Ridge** gave Ron something of a wake-up call. He took the conversation of the lagging numbers as a personal affront. Ron was not used to having to take the blame for anything, but he didn't have any of his go-to scapegoats in the room during the meeting.

Shortly after the meeting, he had yet another owners' conference for the Independent Dealers' Association (IDA). Upon his return, he had his assistant, Shirley, call a meeting of all department managers. The meeting included Ron, Shirley, Darcy, Ted, Daryl, and Bryan Long, the vice president of the service department. Darcy couldn't even begin to wonder what the meeting was about. The management team at Burgess was anything but a team. When Ron wanted to communicate to them, he usually did it individually. A meeting with the group was something new.

When they all gathered in the conference room, they had a few minutes to chat before Ron made his entrance. Daryl immediately turned to Shirley and asked, "Shirley, can you shed light on what this is all about? Is he going to fire all of us?"

Shirley laughed and said, "I doubt that. My guess is that he's come back with one of his ideas from the dealers' association."

Bryan sighed, and said, "Oh, my god. I'm still dealing with the aftermath of the last 'great idea.' How come they always affect me more than anyone else?"

"Because you have the most people in your department and you let Ron lead you around by your nose," laughed Darcy.

Bryan was Darcy's favorite person at Burgess. Ten years earlier, he had been hired as a young delivery driver. She had watched him work his way through almost every job on the service side of the company, finally earning the title of vice president. Bryan's employees loved him, but he, like every other manager in the company, did everything in their power to avoid confrontation with Ron. Therefore, Bryan's department did not live up to their potential. Bryan had tried to make the technicians more accountable, but, for some reason, Ron had stifled every one of his ideas. After several months of hitting the wall, Bryan fell into the under-the-radar mode—where everyone who worked for Ron eventually settled.

Ron sauntered into the meeting five minutes late and immediately started talking. "I know all of you are wondering why I called this meeting. Well, you know I was at the dealers' association last week, and we were presented with an idea that I want to implement immediately." At that, all the managers and Shirley stared down at the table almost in unison, and all tried hard to mask their amusement.

"This group will now be called the Senior Management Team, or SMT for short," Ron stated with pride. "From now on we will get out of our silos, and together we will make all the major decisions for the company. We will bring all the challenges of our departments to the group and together we will discuss and together we will make decisions. No one should hesitate voicing opposition. We want free and open conversation."

It was obvious that everyone else in the room was thinking the same thing by the looks on each of their faces. Not uncharacteristically, Daryl was the first to speak for everyone. "So, Ron, where the heck is this coming from?" They could all see that Ron was a bit perturbed by Daryl's tone, but he let it go.

"Well, for a while I've been realizing that we haven't been working together as a team. I feel that it is having a negative effect on the company. At our meeting last week, Patrick Lencioni spoke about his book, *The Five Dysfunctions of a Team*. I couldn't help but think of this team while he talked."

Darcy chimed in immediately. "I've read his book. It's good, and an easy read. And you are right, Ron. We are very similar to the group of managers that were portrayed in the book. Let's see: we have lack of trust, fear of conflict, lack of commitment to common goals, avoidance of accountability, and concentration on personal success before team success. I'm not saying it's just us, but these are common themes throughout the organization. Ron, this is a heavy lift. It's very difficult to suddenly instill trust in people who have been given no reason to trust in the past."

Ron looked a little shocked at Darcy's directness, but also realized this is what he was looking for. "You are right Darcy. It might take some time to get it right, but I would like a commitment from this group to at least give it a try. We are facing some steep financial challenges, and it's going to take all of us working together to move to the next level. Next Thursday, we are going off-site for a day-long meeting where we are going to air out some of the roadblocks we're all facing. All I'm asking is for everyone to be honest and forthcoming. I also want everyone to remember that this is a meeting on how to improve our company, and nothing said should be taken personally."

When they left the meeting, Bryan made a beeline into Darcy's office and shut the door. "What the hell, Darcy?"

Darcy motioned toward Ron's office as if to remind Bryan of the thin walls. "Is he in there?" she asked.

"No, he left the building as soon as the meeting was over," Bryan answered. "Who knows where he went."

Darcy paused for a moment and chose her words very carefully. "Well Bryan, this caught me off guard as much as it did you, and judging from the looks on everyone else's faces, we all were surprised. We all know that everything Ron has done in the past has had a hidden agenda behind it, but I'd love to hope that maybe he is starting to realize that this ship is going to sink unless he starts making some big changes. This, if he's being honest about the intent, would be a big step toward making a better company."

"I don't know Darcy. I still don't trust him," said Bryan.

"Why don't we give this a shot, Bryan. I mean we really don't have anything to lose. I think the meeting next week will tell a lot about how this thing is going to work. If Ron comes in and tries to control the whole process, then we know that nothing is going to change. Frankly, I don't believe it's in his nature to do it any other way, but let's hope I'm wrong."

"Okay, I'm on board. But I'm like you: I'll believe it when I see it," he said as he headed for her door.

*We will see*, she thought hopefully.

They met at eight o'clock the following Thursday morning in a conference room at a local hotel. Ron had been behind closed doors almost the entire time since the meeting the previous week. They all speculated to each other that, as always, Ron was planning the entire meeting himself and they would be relegated to an entire day of "The Ron Show." The man loved to hear himself pontificate on how things should be.

Ron was the first to arrive, and had set up the room so they were all facing a large whiteboard. On the board, one word was written: "Trust." Once everyone was settled Ron started the discussion.

"Okay, what I would like to do is start today by discussing why there is so little trust within our organization."

Everyone in the room fidgeted a bit because no one "trusted" that it would not be held against them if they answered the question honestly. Finally, Daryl spoke up.

"To be honest, Ron, I believe the lack of trust needs to be laid at your feet. I hate to speak for others, but there seems to be a sense from the people who work for you that they cannot voice any opposition to you without fear of reprisal." Outwardly, Ron did not show any reaction to what Daryl just said. He took a marker and wrote under the word "Trust":

## 1. Inability to voice opposition

Since Daryl's response was met with no hostility, the group started to feel more confident.

Bryan spoke up. "My lack of trust is due to the fact that I will get your agreement on ways I can make the service technicians accountable, and then you reverse me at my service meetings in front of my staff."

At that, Darcy added, "Yes, the same has happened to me where I'll get your agreement, and then you reverse me in front of a group. Not only does it cause lack of trust, but it's humiliating." Ron didn't say a word, but wrote on the board:

## 2. Undermining in front of staff and/or other departments

At that, Ted jumped into the fray. "Darcy and I have tried hard to improve the inventory turns, and every time we think we are on track, you or Bob do something to affect inventory without saying a word to either of us. It makes us look foolish to the staff and hurts our credibility. A stone-faced Ron moved to the whiteboard and wrote:

## 3. Actions that affect a department aren't communicated before they happen

Then Daryl said, "Just to build on what Ted said—communications from you and Bob are severely lacking." Ron wrote on the board:

## 4. Communications are lacking

Ron then turned to the group and asked, "Anything else?" Everyone looked at each other shaking their heads. "Okay, let's move on. We next need to find out why there tends to be an avoidance to express these opinions to either Bob or me." He turned and wrote on the board, "Avoidance of Conflict," and put a bullet point under it. "Who would like to start?" Bryan and Ted both looked at the floor in the hope that they would not have to start the conversation. They were saved when Daryl once again weighed in.

"Well, Ron, I have to say that I'm not one to avoid conflict."

At that Ron rolled his eyes and said, "You can say that again."

"However," Daryl continued, "I can certainly see why there is an aversion. In my case, my conflict does nothing but hurt my cause. It seems the more I try to affect change, the more pushback I get from you. It's extremely frustrating."

At that, Darcy decided to add, "I agree. I tried my best to bring ideas that I felt would be beneficial to the company and they fell on deaf ears. I finally decided it really wasn't worth the trouble, because everything I tried got shot down."

Then Ted spoke up. "Ron, there is a general feeling throughout the company that if someone disagrees with you, they will be hurting their standing with the organization. I believe there are some who actually think they will be fired."

Bryan finally blurted out, "I think Ted is right."

At that, Ron just stared at everyone trying to compose himself. He had thought that this meeting might be a little uncomfortable but was not prepared for the onslaught he had just suffered.

"Okay," he started, "it sounds like we have a lot to discuss. However, I believe that our meeting each week and discussing everyone's ideas with the whole group will remedy a lot of this. And, more importantly, will help us make decisions as a group."

"What I am hearing is that there won't be any inventory buys or departmental policy changes unless it is first discussed with the group," said Darcy. "I recognize that Bob isn't here, and he's perfectly within his rights to do what he wants to do. But will everything else be run before this group before implementation?"

"Absolutely," said Ron.

"Okay," said Darcy, "let's give this a try."

Next on the agenda was a discussion of every employee in the company. Ron wanted to identify who the A, B, and C players were. The idea was to come up with a plan to start compensating the A and B employees based upon merit, as opposed to seniority as was done in the past. The C employees would be put on performance improvement plans. If their quality of work did not improve, they would be terminated.

The discussion started with the admin and accounting departments. Everyone agreed that all staff in those departments scored either an A or a B. Next, they moved to the service department. Here there was much more discussion. Bryan, to his credit, was quite critical of the lower-performing guys in the field. He was at an advantage because he had objective criteria by which to measure his people. Daryl also voiced some negative comments toward a few of the technicians, due to feedback that had come to him through the sales department.

Ron, however, was mostly opposed to giving any of the technicians, even the ones who consistently performed poorly against the benchmarks, a C rating. He finally said, "There's something you all have to understand. We have the most experienced group of service technicians in the state. If we start getting rid of some of these guys, how are we going to replace them? Plus, you know they will end up working for our competitors."

Daryl quickly responded, "Ron, with all due respect, I don't understand that rationale at all. If they are bad employees, then I would prefer that they work for a competitor. As for how to replace them, we are the best dealership in the state. My guess is that we could hire away some of our competitors' guys."

He shot a look at Bryan, who said quickly, "Daryl's right. I get inquiries all of the time."

Ron looked at them skeptically. "Okay, we obviously have some disagreement here. Let's hold this discussion for a later meeting and move on to the warehouse. I think we have a solid team right now. What are your thoughts?"

Darcy was the first to speak up. "For the most part, I agree. However, Ron, you and Ted both know my feelings about how weak of a manager Clint is. I think he is very knowledgeable about our business and was once a great employee, but he is not, and never was or will be, a good candidate for management."

Darcy could see a flash of anger in Ron's face. She had pushed too far. It didn't help that her colleagues were being noticeably silent. Either they didn't agree, or they too had seen the change in Ron's demeanor. Perhaps they had pressed their luck with all this newfound openness. Finally, Ted, of all people, jumped in to rescue Darcy.

"I'm sorry Ron, but I must agree with Darcy. Clint has been nothing but trouble since I took over that department. He fights me at every turn. Quite frankly, if I hear, 'Are you sure that's okay with Ron?' one more time, I think I'm going to scream."

Darcy couldn't believe what she was hearing. The doormat—Ted—was going after Ron's guy with a vengeance. Suddenly, it was clear that Ron had enough.

"I'm sorry guys but I'm going to pull rank here. We are going to table the discussion on Clint." Darcy, Daryl, Ted and Bryan shot glances to each other indicating a realization that Ron's new attitude was fragile. Perhaps they should slow down. Rome wasn't built in a day.

When the discussion turned to the sales department, Daryl did not go off on the reps in Greensboro and Raleigh. He instead said that he wanted to reserve conversation on the sales department in general for another meeting. "We've come up with a lot to chew on. I think it would be best to tackle sales later," he said. Everyone expressed their opinion by quickly agreeing in the affirmative.

The remaining conversation had to do with ground rules and meeting times. Darcy expressed her pleasure with the concept, and thanked Ron for coming up with the idea. "I really feel like this will move the company forward. My only request is that we all make these meetings a priority. I feel that it is crucial that we all understand the importance of this."

Ron looked at her dismissively, "Darcy I think that goes without saying."

Over the next few weeks, the SMT met first thing on Monday morning to discuss all issues, and made all the important decisions as Ron had promised. Darcy and the other managers were very happy with the direction in which the company was beginning to move. When possible, they would meet for lunch after the meeting to further discuss any topics they felt Ron was avoiding. Though he had kept his promise to have an open forum, he continued to control the agenda. For that reason, the conversation had not gravitated back toward the personnel issues that were plaguing both Ted and Daryl.

One Monday, about three months after the initial meeting, Daryl, Darcy, Ted, and Bryan were at lunch. Daryl was becoming increasingly agitated that Ron kept putting off the discussion of sales compensation. Each week when Daryl gave his report, he asked if it would be a good time for the discussion. Each week, Ron deferred using a lack of time as the excuse.

"I'm beginning to feel like Ron is losing interest in our mission," Daryl said. "I want to get this sales situation rectified, but it's almost as if Ron is avoiding it."

"Not "as if"; he's absolutely avoiding it," said Darcy. "He knows that the rest of us are going to agree with you. Forcing him to loosen his grip on the sales department is going to be the ultimate act of defiance in his eyes. Instead of confronting that defiance, he is choosing to avoid it altogether."

Eventually, the managers noticed that Ron was beginning to make the agenda shorter and shorter. Meetings that lasted almost two hours in the beginning were now lasting less than an hour. In addition, Ron began to schedule trips that had him at the airport first thing on Monday, so meetings began to be cancelled. This was a significant blow to Darcy. She had loved the original idea and had learned so much about the other departments during this time. While the other managers were on board, it appeared that they were losing Ron quickly.

The managers began to routinely meet off-site for lunch on Monday to conduct a mini-SMT meeting to discuss the items that Ron had made off limits. Each department had at least one major concern. The managers began to compile a list, which they could refer to if they ever had the opportunity to get Ron's attention.

For Daryl, of course, the major concern was the fairness of the sales compensation and his highly-paid, underperforming reps. Bryan's concern also had to do with compensation. He had wanted to implement a bonus plan for the technicians based upon how they were performing against benchmarks that measured the efficiency of each of their service calls. He also wanted to make the techs accountable for poor performance, anywhere from withholding annual raises to termination. Ted's concerns had to do with Clint's performance as a manager and the lack of control he had over inventory.

Darcy's admin group had recently discovered that almost all the service contracts on their highest dollar machines were not only losing money, but were losing a lot of money. When she confronted Ron about it in one of their recent SMT meetings, he said that the structure of the contract was necessary to be able to compete in the market for the high-end equipment. The margins to place those machines were very thin, so normally it would stand to reason that they would rely on the service revenue to cover the investment in the inventory. Darcy was having trouble understanding the purpose of competing in that segment if they couldn't make money. However, Ron's concern was the loss of top-line revenue. Like the rest of the managers' concerns, Ron finally took discussion of these contracts off the table.

Finally, the situation with the managed services division was not improving at a quick enough rate. It was clear that they needed to make some drastic changes. The consensus of the group was if they were going to stay in the IT services business, they needed to start looking for an acquisition.

The group felt that Ron avoided discussion of this simply because he felt that doing so would admit failure. Everyone began to feel confident that if they could get Ron out of the way, they could make tremendous strides in the performance of the company.

Several months into the SMT project, when meetings had become virtually non-existent, Ron decided that they would take on a new mission. First, they would change their name from the SMT to the SLT (Senior Leadership Team). He felt that it sounded less imposing to the employees.

When he announced the new name, the rest of the "team" all looked at each other in disbelief. Now, when they had real action items to be dealt with that could move the company forward, Ron had been concerning himself with how the name sounded to the employees. Ron had decided it was time that they come up with the company's core values. He scheduled a retreat for the group so they could spend a couple of days off site where they would all have input into the process without interruption.

# WHOSE CORE
# VALUES?

**Ron found a golf resort/corporate retreat** a few hours east of Charlotte near the Nantahala River for their meeting. While Ron was not a golfer, he knew the rest of the group loved the game. He felt a round of golf for the four of them would be a great team builder.

In addition to the golf, Ron arranged a raft trip on the river. During their mini-SLT lunch two days before the trip, they all decided to go into the exercise with an open mind. None of them knew for sure where Ron had suddenly gotten the idea to change directions with the SLT (or SMT), but they guessed it came from one of Ron's buddies at the dealers' association.

The retreat was a beautiful, rustic lodge near the Great Smoky Mountains National Park. The conference room that they were given had floor to ceiling windows that overlooked the eighteenth hole on the golf course. None of them had a clue as to how they were expected to concentrate on company core values.

The plan for the first day was to work during the morning and play golf after lunch. Not knowing what to expect, the group headed in after breakfast and took their seats at the huge conference table. Daryl, Darcy, Ted, and Bryan all took seats facing the large window overlooking the golf course. Shirley took a seat on the other side of the table, assuming Ron would want to face the managers.

Ron came in about five minutes later and immediately walked to a large white flip chart that had been pushed to the side of the room. He moved it in front of the group, blocking Bryan's view of the golf course. When Ron turned his back, Bryan grimaced, forcing everyone to stifle a laugh.

"Why don't we jump right in since we only have a few hours before we break?" Ron started. "How many of you have ever been involved in writing the core values of an organization?" Everyone sat quietly with blank stares on their faces.

Already knowing the answer, Daryl asked, "So, Ron, have you ever done this?"

"Well, not exactly, Daryl," Ron answered. "But I have sat in on several meetings in which writing core values was the topic. That's why I took the liberty of jotting down a few ideas of what I feel Burgess's core values should look like. Not that this is etched in stone, it's more of a starting point."

At that, Ron turned the first page of the flip chart. Before them was not only a list of core values, but also descriptions under each that told why they were important to Burgess.

Half joking, Darcy said, "Ron, I thought we were going to do this exercise together. It looks to me like you've already taken care of it. Maybe we can get thirty-six holes in before dinner." At that, everyone laughed. Everyone, that is, except Ron.

"If you guys are finished goofing around," said Ron with irritation in his voice. "As I said, Darcy, this is just the beginning. I wanted to give you my vision on how these would look."

As they all focused their attention on the chart, they each began to silently read Ron's vision:

- **Trust** – We believe that trust and respect are essential for teamwork.

- **Communication** – We believe in open and honest communication.

- **Respect** – We value and respect every member of the team and encourage their development.

- **Community** – We believe that giving back to the community is our way to be positive role models for others.

- **Frugality** – We believe in doing more with less.

- **Integrity** – We are committed to high standards and integrity.

Everyone from the team was speechless. Was Ron kidding? Where in the world did he get these core values? They certainly did not reflect the values of Burgess.

As always, Daryl was the first to speak. Choosing his words carefully he said, "Ron, I appreciate the time you put into this. But in my opinion, if we took anything like this back to the employees, they would laugh us out of the room. I understand that this is what you would like to see, but honestly, we are far from most of it."

Darcy was next to speak. "Ron, I think forming a company's core values is something that needs to evolve. I've read that the companies that ignore their core values and instead concentrate on what it is that makes the company great are much more successful in coming up with a vision that all employees buy in to. I'm not saying that all of those are off-base. For instance, I think there is a high level of integrity amongst our staff. I also think, for the most part, our employees respect each other. My vote would be to get rid of the "trust" and "communication" values until we can prove to everyone that we have changed."

Ron flashed Darcy a look of contempt, saying: "You guys have made it abundantly clear that we are totally devoid of trust, and communication pretty much sucks. But the bottom line is that those are two values that are present in a very large percentage of successful companies. In my opinion, it is very important that we include them in ours."

"But it's a lie," Ted blurted out. Everyone stared at Ted in disbelief. To their surprise, Ron's head didn't explode. In fact, he calmly responded to Ted.

"Ted, I understand what you are saying, but we've spent the last few months committing ourselves to being more honest and trying to improve communications. I think we've come a long way." At that, Ted shook his head, closed his notebook, and visibly disengaged from the conversation.

"Who else would like to give their input?" Ron asked. The silence was palpable.

The rest of the morning session consisted of Ron going more in depth about each of the core values. There were very few comments after Ted was shot down; "The Ron Show" was in full swing. The four managers could all be seen glancing at their watches, counting the minutes until they were free to hit the golf course.

Once the meeting was adjourned, they headed to the golf course, while Ron and Shirley stayed at the lodge to finalize the plans for the rafting trip the following day. They were to meet for dinner following their golf game at the outside balcony restaurant.

"My god, how excruciating was that?" Bryan asked as they headed for their golf carts. "I swear I almost jumped through one of those windows just to put myself out of my misery."

"Guys, seriously, what are we going to do?" asked Ted. "Ron has no clue what the employees think of him. In fact, hearing him talk today, I believe he really thinks they all look up to him as a mentor. How could anyone be that dense?"

"That's a very good question, Ted," said Daryl. "What *are* we going to do? We can't take this rubbish back to the employees."

"I was thinking about that," said Darcy, "We need to get him to rein this in, and make him think it was his idea."

"How are we going to do that?" asked Bryan.

"Well, I think what we need to do is let him know that we are completely on board with his ideas, but start giving some different ideas on the roll-out," said Darcy.

"Yeah, like waiting until the year we all retire," said Bryan.

"That wouldn't be a bad idea for me, because I'm old," Darcy said. "But since you are something like twelve, we may have a problem. Seriously, I think we need to strategize on how to delay this without completely pissing him off."

"Wait," Ted said with excitement, "I've got an idea. Why don't we convince him to wait to roll it out in conjunction with our thirtieth anniversary? That's not until next summer; that gives us a year to figure out what to do. Who knows, one of us may be able to come up with some real core values that will completely wow him." He looked at the stone-faced stares of the other managers and said, "Or not."

They had a great day on the golf course. Daryl and Darcy rode together in the cart, and spent the entire round discussing the many ways they could make a difference if they had any authority whatsoever. It was particularly frustrating for the two of them, because both had management backgrounds in companies much more successful than Burgess. They both knew how an effective management team worked and how important they were to the ultimate success of the company.

Prior to moving to the office products industry, Daryl had led sales teams twice the size as Burgess's. He had proven records of double-digit growth in every engagement as the sales manager until he came to Burgess. This year the company would be lucky to reach last year's mark. More than likely, they would end the year down 1-2 percent. That really pissed Daryl off.

Darcy's background was with a small subsidiary of a Fortune 500 company. Their management team had lofty expectations from the main office and, out of necessity, they had to come up with a process that maximized profits for the big wigs in Charlotte. They knew progress was being made when they heard nothing from the home office. It was only when the profits began to slip at their level that the company would send in the internal auditors to make sure everything was being done the right way. The synergy within their management team was exhilarating. They quickly became the rock stars among the subsidiary offices, so strong that they all worked themselves out of a job.

Eventually, a large competitor approached the company about an acquisition. Within three months, their subsidiary was sold, and the management team was offered a severance package, which gave Darcy an opportunity to take time to search for her ideal gig. About that time, her old friend Bob called and offered her a job with his company. That had been seventeen years earlier. Darcy didn't know whether she had gotten lazy, or had just let her position at Burgess become her identity. Two things were for certain: (1) the time spent at Burgess had done very little to advance her career, and (2) she should have parted ways with the company several years earlier. However, it really had been a lot of fun until Bob exited the scene.

After the round of golf, the group had time for one drink in the bar before they headed up to the lodge to get ready for dinner. As they sat around the table, they discussed their action plan to convince Ron that they should delay the roll-out of the core values.

"Well I definitely think it should come from Bryan," said Darcy. She looked straight at him and said, "he likes you best."

"No way, not gonna do it," Bryan said defiantly. "You're right, he likes me. I would really like to keep it that way. That's the easiest way to stay under the radar."

He then turned to Ted and said, "You lost the match today, dude. I'll forego the twenty bucks I won playing golf if you'll do this. Darcy's right; it should be someone Ron likes. And with all due respect to you, Darcy and Daryl, he really hates both of you."

"I wear it like a badge of honor," Daryl said.

Dinner was pleasant. When he wasn't trying to be the boss, Ron really could be a lot of fun outside of the office. Though there was no shop talk, they joked about some of the interesting employees and crazy customers they had endured over the years. Nothing was said about the meeting that morning, which was a blessing. It would have certainly put a damper on what had turned out to be a very good afternoon. As they finished dinner and began to head back to their rooms, Ron suggested they all get a good night's sleep; they were scheduled to leave for the river at seven thirty the next morning. Bryan and Darcy looked at each other and rolled their eyes.

When they met in the lobby in the morning, Darcy barely had time to grab a cup of coffee. She loved outdoor adventures, but this morning was a little difficult, because of the several glasses of wine she had consumed the night before. She climbed onto the bus and made a beeline to the back, planning to sleep the entire hour it would take for them to get to the river.

As they pulled away from the hotel, much to Darcy's chagrin, Ron popped up in front of the group and began to give a rundown of the morning's adventure.

"Darcy, can you please move up to the front, so I only have to go over this one time?" he asked. She shot him a look of disdain, dragged herself to the front of the bus, and plopped down beside Ted.

"Okay, what is so important that it is going to take me away from my beauty sleep?" she moaned. "Which I am in dire need of."

For the next half-hour, Ron droned on about the rules and regulations while rafting on the river. He also talked about what made this an important team building exercise. Last, he went over the agenda for the afternoon meeting: more about core values. Darcy certainly hoped that there would be coffee provided in the conference room. If not, there was no way she was going to be able to stay awake.

The group had to hand it to Ron, the rafting trip was something to behold. The scenery they witnessed as they floated down the river was quite stunning. For the most part, the trip was uneventful, but there were a few times when they really did have to work as a team to navigate through some of the rough waters. About halfway through, they hit a rock and Ted was catapulted from one side of the raft to the other. Had he gone a few feet further, he would have been in the river's cold waters.

Lance, the tour guide, tried to calm the visibly shaken Ted by saying, "Ted, you are one of the lucky ones. We lose one over the side about once a week." His words were of little comfort to Ted.

The bus ride back to the lodge was much quieter. Ron decided to give everyone a break and let them rest. A few hours on the river spent in the sun and heat had taken its toll. Practically everyone was asleep within minutes of boarding.

When they reached the lodge, they were given box lunches and about forty-five minutes to shower and then make their way to the conference room. When Daryl arrived five minutes early, Ron and Shirley were already there setting up the room. Soon after, Ted and Bryan walked in. Darcy was a fashionable five minutes late, with coffee in hand. Everyone found the same seats they had occupied the day before, and prepared for another agonizing multi-hour meeting.

Ron began the meeting by restating the "decisions" that had been made the day before regarding the core values. At that, Ted chimed in.

"Ron, I was thinking. We have had several discussions over the past few months about next year's thirtieth anniversary. Wouldn't that be a great opportunity to roll out our new core values? I'm sure there will be some re-branding to incorporate the thirty years. At the same time, we could announce to the world our newly minted core values. Meanwhile, that will give us time to refine and make sure we are putting forth something that really expresses the company's true values."

At that, Darcy spoke up. "Ron, I think that's a great idea. Also, I had a thought. I would be interested in knowing what the employees feel make up our core values. We may get some great ideas from some of them if we ask. We could do a survey and work with the best and most frequent responses."

Ron was visibly annoyed by the turn the project had taken. He had come out of yesterday's meeting confident that his outline was a good first draft. Now everything was being changed. He had already sent the outline to the guys in marketing to come up with some boards with ideas on how to present the core values.

"I really wish we had discussed this yesterday," he said. "I've already got Jim in marketing working on it."

"Sorry, Ron, but I didn't think of it until yesterday afternoon," said Ted.

"So, what are you going to do, Ron?" asked Daryl.

"I think we will wait to see what Jim comes back with and table this discussion until that time," said Ron. The group knew what that meant. Once the presentation came back from marketing, the core values would be as good as written in stone.

The rest of the meeting consisted of Ron telling everyone how the company would use the core values in their everyday dealing with both employees and customers. Employee evaluations would have to be changed to assess how well an employee expressed the values in the way they conducted themselves on the job. The group of managers silently listened as Ron once again ran the show. It was easier to nod their heads in agreement than to attempt to interject something that he would most likely shoot down. After the meeting, with hardly a word of goodbye, they all quickly headed for their cars to make the three and one-half hour trip home. *What a waste*, Darcy thought. Ron could have saved the company a lot of money by just admitting he did not have the capacity to value the opinion of others.

At the very next SLT meeting, Ron proudly unveiled the board the Marketing department had come up with to display Burgess's (Ron's) core values. They had done a very impressive job. As the managers sat and looked at the colorful poster, they were almost convinced that the words so prominently displayed in a circle on the board really were Burgess's core values.

As they had assumed, the "tabled" discussion was never "un-tabled." Since the design was so compelling, Ron decided that the employee meeting the following month would be a great time to introduce the new core values. They all just rolled their eyes and said nothing.

The morning of the next employee meeting, the four managers stood in the back of the room so they could get a good look at the reaction from the employees. As Ron stood in front of everyone proudly talking about the team process they had gone through to come up with the core values, Darcy let out an audible sigh. If Ron heard it, he ignored her. Once he was finished with his explanation of core values and how important they were to a company, he brought Jim up to show the handiwork of the marketing department.

When the large board was uncovered all the employees immediately began to clap in reaction to the beautiful artwork. They then began to read the words. Some employees continued to be excited for the company's new core values, while others stared at the words as if they couldn't believe what they were reading. Daryl heard one of the technicians standing in the back swear under his breath, "Are they f-ing kidding?" He then began to laugh. Daryl looked over at Darcy and just smiled. More than half of the people in the room were visibly unimpressed. They just shook their heads and left the room as soon as it was comfortable to do so.

Over the next few weeks, the posters began popping up throughout the building, as well as at the branch offices. It really was quite impressive to customers who visited. Almost all commented on how great they looked, and how commendable the values were.

Meanwhile, not much had changed operationally. Trust was still non-existent; communication still sucked.

# COMMUNITY OUTREACH

**One area Ron felt they needed to work on** to conform with their new core values was in community outreach. Burgess had a history of occasionally sponsoring holes for local golf tournaments and giving minimal amounts to customers who asked them to give to a favorite charity. Ron wanted Burgess to make a name for itself as a leader in community outreach.

He heard that Janet Simpson, one of Betty's customer service reps, had a background working with non-profits, along with a passion for doing so. Ron thought she would be the perfect person to head up the initiative. One day, he called Janet to his office to discuss his plans.

Ron's vision was to create a community outreach division, which would sponsor golf tournaments, 5K and 10K races, and, most importantly, would target local underfunded charities to become a benefactor through holding fundraising campaigns. A couple of the much larger owners of the Independent Dealers' Association had gone so far as to start their own 501(c)3s. Ron desperately wanted that for Burgess.

When Janet left Ron's office, she was pumped. This was exactly what she wanted. She headed for Betty's office. "Betty thank you so much for the opportunity," she said as she entered. Betty glanced up at her with a puzzled look on her face.

"Excuse me, but what opportunity?"

"The community outreach position; Ron just told me all about it. I've got so many ideas already."

Betty just stared at her and said, "Janet, I have no idea what you are talking about. What community outreach position?"

"He just offered me a job as our new Community Outreach Coordinator. I'm not sure when it's going to start, but my guess is he's going to give us time to find my replacement."

Betty stood up and said, "Janet, you'll need to excuse me, but I need to go and talk to Darcy. I've got to find out what's going on here."

Betty walked into Darcy's office and closed the door. "What are you guys trying to do to me?" she asked. Darcy looked up to see a very agitated Betty.

"What do you mean, Betty?" asked Darcy.

"Janet came into my office and said Ron had just offered her another job," she said, going on to describe the conversation she'd just had with Betty. "I think she said, 'Community Outreach Coordinator.' Isn't it customary to talk to an employee's manager before you go and poach them?"

"Betty, I honestly have no idea what you are talking about," said Darcy.

Betty shook her head and said, "Why am I not surprised? I was having trouble believing you would have done this without telling me."

"Listen, Betty, I'll talk to Ron and find out what is going on," said Darcy. "Something doesn't sound right. This seems a little extreme, even for Ron."

Darcy found Ron at his desk staring at his computer. He looked up and asked, "What's up?"

"Ron, I just talked to Betty, and she's very upset," she answered. He genuinely looked like he had no idea why. "Did you offer Janet another job without talking to Betty?"

"No," he said adamantly, "I asked her to be our Community Outreach Coordinator, but that is a volunteer position. She'll still be expected to do her job."

"Okay Ron, there has been a huge misunderstanding here," said Darcy. "Janet is under the impression that what you offered her is a full-time job that she will get paid for. According to Betty, she's making all kinds of plans for fundraisers and golf tournaments."

"Oh no," said Ron, "you know as well as I do that we can't afford that."

Darcy just stared at him refusing to voice agreement to something so obvious. "Good grief, Ron," she said. "What are you going to do about this? Janet's a good employee. This will crush her."

"I'll just have to make clear to her what I meant," he said. "She can decide to either do it or not."

"Ron, can you please do me a favor?" she asked. "The next time you talk to one of my employees about something like this, could you please give me a heads-up first? Betty is now more than likely going to have to deal with a morale issue. This was all so unnecessary!"

"Darcy, I can talk to anyone I want at any time. It's not my fault that Janet misunderstood what I said to her," he said.

Darcy rolled her eyes and turned to leave his office before she said something she would regret. "Okay, but could you please talk to Janet as soon as possible?" she asked.

Janet was clearly upset after Ron talked to her a second time. She told Betty that as much as she wanted to take on the extra work, she just didn't feel with her job duties she could devote the time that would do it justice. Ron's expectations were quite high.

To Darcy's surprise, Betty encouraged Janet to give it a try and see if she could make it work. Betty felt the only way she could salvage Janet after such a big disappointment was to try to support and accommodate her as much as possible. She knew there was a huge risk that job performance would drop, but she felt she had been given no choice.

As the new initiative took form, Ron decided there needed to be a better presence for Burgess Outreach, as the initiative had been named. He got the marketing department working full time on putting together a website and booked Janet to speak at networking events in the evening.

One Monday morning Ron asked Janet to give a presentation on her progress to the SLT. She went on about the different fund-raising efforts they were participating in. She was particularly proud of the new charity they had found to support. The company had committed to preparing bags of food each week for needy families.

To Darcy, it sounded like a lot of work for everyone since employees would be asked to volunteer to get the job completed each week.

"When will they be putting together these bags?" asked Darcy.

Ron jumped in and said, "We've set aside a couple of hours every day. Employees can jump into the assembly line during their breaks and lunch hours."

"I don't mean to throw cold water on this valiant effort," said Darcy, "but we just don't have that many people in the office during the day. How do we know we will get enough people to volunteer? One of the worst things that can happen is if we over-promise and under-deliver."

Janet spoke up, "Darcy, I really don't think that will be a problem. Our people love to volunteer their time."

Darcy wasn't convinced. Maybe if they had double the number of people in the office during the day they could get it done. She felt certain this was going to fall on the shoulders of the admin and warehouse staff. This was going to get old fast. "Okay," she finally said, "I hope you are right."

Janet was working forty hours a week and "volunteering" another ten. Pretty soon, as Burgess Outreach became more well-known, the personal appearances for Janet began to be earlier and earlier in the day. Late one afternoon Betty showed up at Darcy's door. She looked tired.

"What's wrong Betty?" Darcy asked.

"Darcy, I may have made a mistake on this Janet situation. I'm killing myself helping her keep up with her work. Now she is coming to me wanting me to see if we can start paying her overtime for all the extra work. I told her that Ron made it clear that this is a volunteer position. I told her we just couldn't afford it. She wasn't happy about that."

"Betty, I believe you should stop covering for Janet," said Darcy. "She needs to keep up with her work if she's going to do this volunteer job. You need to start pushing back. I believe this thing has gotten way too big, way too fast. We have a lot to do, and this is too much of a distraction."

A few days later Ron showed up at Darcy's office. "Darcy, I think we need to talk about what we are going to do about Janet. We are finding that we need her a lot more for the outreach, and we've decided to start a 501(c)3, so she's going to be working hard to navigate that."

"I'm sorry, Ron," Darcy said, "but I'm not sure what you mean. I do know that Betty is increasingly worried that Janet is losing interest in her job. Betty has been working hard to cover for Janet since she's been pulled away from the office more recently."

"I know. Janet came to me the other day saying that Betty had rejected the idea that she gets paid for her overtime for the outreach initiative. Darcy, I'm beginning to believe we should start paying her for her efforts. We are really starting to get some traction." Darcy looked at him in disbelief.

"Ron, you and I agreed a few weeks ago that we can't afford to pay anyone for this outreach. It needs to be 100 percent volunteer."

"Yes, we did Darcy, so I think I have come up with a solution. You know Abby, our receptionist, has been trying to get an interview with Betty for a position in her department. What if we were to switch Janet and Abby? That would give Janet more time to do her outreach job, and Abby would get an opportunity to be a customer service rep."

"I'm not sure how that would work," said Darcy. "If we adjust Janet's rate commensurate to that of a receptionist, there is no way she would make the money she is expecting."

"I'm not suggesting that," said Ron. "We'll keep Janet at her current rate. The reduction in job duties will give her more time to work on the outreach."

"But Ron, we are still going to need to cover for Janet when she is pulled away from the receptionist desk. How is that going to work?"

"One of the admin people will fill in when needed," said Ron. All Darcy could think, was that would fly like a lead balloon.

Betty was livid when she heard the news. "Darcy, there is a reason that I haven't given Abby an interview," she said. "It's because she isn't qualified for the job. I'm going to spend more time getting her up to speed than I did covering for Janet. Also, my admin staff is already worn out because Janet is constantly urging them to help pack grocery bags in every spare minute. At first, they were excited about it, but since they are the only ones doing it each day, it's getting old. Now you are telling me that they are going to start covering for Janet at the reception desk? Darcy, I love what we are trying to do here, but that isn't what we are here for. I thought we were trying to run a business. There is so much value we could bring to the community without committing so much time. Part of the reason to do this is for the pleasure the employees get from helping. I can tell you it is becoming more of a chore than anything."

Within a couple of months, Ron realized that having admin cover for Janet was becoming a problem with morale. Janet told him that they were volunteering less for the food packing effort, and there were only a few people now who consistently helped; Janet was working extra time just to fulfill their weekly commitment. Ron decided that the solution would be to hire a part-time receptionist to work in the afternoon. That would free up Janet without imposing on the admin department. Darcy thought about how expensive this "all-volunteer" initiative was becoming.

Janet had been working hard to get the 501(c)3 established, which would help in their fundraising efforts. Once that was completed, she began to work on a couple of big events: a golf tournament and a 5K race. There was no question that, by now, the Outreach Coordinator position had become a full-time job. Shortly thereafter, Ron hired a morning receptionist, and Janet was free the entire day to do the work she loved.

SLT meetings began being consumed by planning and discussing outreach efforts. The managers were becoming concerned that they were losing sight of the core business. Daryl was particularly concerned that the marketing department had been completely coopted by community outreach.

To his credit, Ron began to see that the managers were not as passionate about the initiative as he and Janet. One day he came in with some big news.

"I know all of you have been concerned with the amount of time and effort that we've all been asked to devote to our outreach division," he started. "I appreciate that you would like to get back to our basic business, and I commend you for that. For that reason, I decided to bring in some help for Janet and me. Some of you may remember Charles Murphy." Charles Murphy was a former salesperson who had left the company a few years earlier to pursue another career, which apparently did not pan out. "I have hired Charles to go out into the community with Janet for our fundraising efforts. He knows a lot of people in town, and should be able to get our name out there a lot faster."

The managers all just stared at Ron in disbelief. Darcy was the first to speak up. "Ron, this thing is starting to get very expensive.

We went from all-volunteer to two paid positions, plus a marketing department committed full time. What is our return here?"

"Darcy, we are getting a lot of positive feedback from people. Our customers love what we are doing."

"No one is disputing that, Ron," said Daryl. "It's just that there are not only the additional hard costs, but there are also the soft costs. Our office staff is already tired of this. I think this thing is much bigger than a company our size can handle."

"Okay, I hear you guys," said Ron, "but I think this is very important. With Charles on board to help Janet, I think things will settle down."

Daryl and Darcy realized they were not being heard. Yet another unnecessary expense they would need to absorb.

# THE NEW DIGS

**One afternoon, Darcy received** a call from Bob. Since his contact with her lately had been the occasional email request to update Great Ridge on the financials, this was a surprise. "Darcy, I want you and Ron to go look at a building that I think I want to buy. We are close to out-growing our current place, and a friend came across this one. It really looks like it would work for us." This was yet another situation where Darcy knew the drill. Bob had threatened to move them several times over the past ten years, but when it came down to the final decision, he had always backed out.

"Have you seen it?" she asked.

"No," he said, "but I've got all the specs and the pictures they sent to me. That gives me a good idea of what it looks like. I want to get your and Ron's opinion."

After the call, Ron and Darcy arranged to meet at the building the next morning. When she pulled up, she was shocked at how nice the outside looked. The buildings that they had been sent to in the past had all been unsightly places that obviously needed a lot of work. When Bob did buy buildings, he usually bought distressed properties. He had a few handymen he employed who worked on his many rental properties, and Bob would usually enlist their help to get the buildings back up to speed.

Darcy had to admit: she was quite intrigued. When Ron pulled up, she got out of her car and walked over to him. "Are we in the right place?" she asked. "This place is way too nice."

Ron laughed and said, "I know, it's beautiful. Let's go in and see what shape the interior is in." Again, to their surprise, the inside was just as nice as the outside. There obviously would be some work to be done, but nothing major. The building was laid out perfectly for their business. They spent the next hour going through the building trying to imagine what it would look like once the necessary changes were made to make it their own. The warehouse was fabulous. Their current facility was not large enough to house all the inventory, so Bob owned a warehouse a few miles away. When equipment was needed to set-up for sale, someone had to drive to the off-site location to get what was needed and transport it back to the main office—by no means the height of efficiency.

When they returned to the office, they called Bob to tell him how impressed they were with the building.

"Bob, I think this one has real potential," said Ron. "There is so much we can do with it. The showroom will be magnificent!"

Bob responded by asking Darcy, "So Darcy, what are your thoughts?"

"I have to admit Bob, as much as I hate moving, this building is the closest thing to perfect we've seen. I love the idea that my team would all be together."

"Great," exclaimed Bob, "because I made an offer earlier today."

At that, Darcy became slightly annoyed. She had no reason to believe that Bob would have allowed his intentions to be swayed by her and Ron, but it would have been nice for him to at least let them believe that they had some input. But she put her disappointment aside and began to think about how nice it would be to have a facility large enough to easily house the entire Charlotte staff.

"Oh, and Darcy," added Bob, "I'm going to send over the details. Can you jump on the financing? It's going to be tight until I can either rent or sell the current office and the warehouse." At this, the red flags started waving for Darcy. Cash was very tight these days, not to mention the fact that the balance sheet had taken a beating the last few years. She wasn't sure if they would be able to find a bank that would take on a large loan unless they could show that they were close on having tenants or buyers for their two current properties.

Darcy contacted every banker she knew to see if she could get any interest. One local bank they had been doing business with for several years decided to take the risk. Once they found out that Bob had substantial equity in a few of his commercial real estate properties, they established liens on the properties and gave Bob a thirty-year mortgage. All of this was done within a few weeks. Then it was just a matter of setting a closing date and trying to find new occupants for the existing offices. Darcy was particularly concerned about this, because she knew they would be expected to come up with the cash for the mortgages on those two buildings until they were sold.

At the next SLT meeting, Ron proudly announced the news about the new building to the other managers. It certainly took everyone by surprise. They all knew that Bob had talked for several years about moving, but just assumed it would never happen. Ron suggested that they meet at the new building the next morning and look at it as a team.

The next morning as they walked through, they all started throwing out ideas on what to do with each section of the building. Darcy heard a lot of great ideas, but also a lot of expensive ideas. Finally, she stopped and said, "We really need to be frugal with this move. I understand we want it to look nice, but I must remind all of you about our cash flow problems. We need to put together a very strict budget."

At that Ron added, "Darcy's correct: we need to go slowly. I've decided to put together a committee to work on the move so none of you will be taken away from your regular job duties."

Darcy did not like the sound of that, and said, "Ron I think this group should be involved in coming up with the budget. You said we should be making the decisions. This move will include some very big decisions."

At that Ron said, "We will come up with a budget and let this group review it. I just don't want all of us getting caught up in this move. We have a company to run."

Throughout the next weeks, Darcy heard rumors of Ron's grand plans for the new office. One day she walked into the admin department only to find a top-of-the-line, motorized, standing desk sitting outside Betty's office. She walked in with a confused look on her face.

"Betty, what is that?"

Betty looked up and said, "I thought you knew about it. It's the prototype for the new desks that will be used in the admin department. Ron thought it would be chic if they all had the newest thing. Darcy, I'm telling you right now, there is no way I'm going to stand up while I work." Darcy couldn't help but be amused. Betty was the last person she could ever imagine at a standing desk.

"Betty, I had no idea," said Darcy. "I'm sure Ron doesn't expect you to have one in your office. However, to be honest, I have no idea what Ron has planned. He and his committee are working in private. I don't even have a budget, so I have no idea how much all of this is going to cost."

Betty frowned, "Darcy, how do you do something this big without a budget? Ron is such a stickler about a lot of things, like overtime and pens and paperclips. Yet on big things like this, he seems to have no problem spending other people's money. Go figure."

"Well to be sure, Betty," said Darcy, "I will certainly go to bat for you; I promise you aren't going to lose your chair."

Darcy had hoped she could discuss the budget for the building at the next SLT meeting, but Ron was back in the habit of cancelling it. Finally, Darcy went to Ron one afternoon and said, "Ron, I know you didn't want me involved in this move, but I saw the expensive desk over in admin, and it reminded me that I have yet to see a budget. Thanks to Bob's last inventory buy, we have some huge vendor bills to pay, and I need to know what this is going to cost."

"Darcy, I understand your concern, but we are negotiating good deals. I just don't think it's going to be that expensive."

"Ron, I hate to sound like a broken record, but could you please send me a budget like you said you would?" asked Darcy.

"Okay, okay, I'll have something to you tomorrow," said Ron.

The next day when Darcy walked into her office, there was an envelope sitting on her desk with some numbers jotted on the back:

- electrical – $15,000
- furniture – $10,000

The note at the bottom said, "Darcy, Bob's handymen will be doing the painting and the physical moving of the furniture. So, I think that's it." *You've got to be kidding me*, thought Darcy. *What kind of budget is this? Does Ron think that the handymen are going to work for free?*

She stormed out of her office heading for Ron's to confront him about the non-budget, but he wasn't there. Shirley was straightening some papers on his desk.

"Where is he?" asked Darcy.

"He left town again this morning," said Shirley. "Can I help you with something?" Darcy shook her head and began to walk out until she suddenly had a thought.

"Shirley, there is something you can do for me. I'm compiling the moving expenses for next year's taxes. I know you see all of Ron's expenses. Can you let me know of anything that looks like it is related to the move?"

"Sure, not a problem," said Shirley. "I know he sometimes uses his personal credit card for things, I guess out of convenience. So, I'll get you those expenses."

"Perfect," said Darcy. "That's exactly what I need."

She immediately called the staff accountant, Ben, and the accounts payable clerk, Jake, into her office. "Okay, guys, I need you to do something for me. We are going to need all the moving expenses for taxes next year. I want you to start compiling a list now, because my guess is that they are going to be coming from several sources. Shirley is going to give us the information on Ron's spending, but I also want you to check expense reports and credit cards. I want to get an accurate accounting of what we really spend."

For the next three months, Ron spent most of his time managing the moving project. Even though the managers would have liked to give some input on the building design, they did appreciate that Ron didn't have anyone in his crosshairs during that time.

As moving day approached, Darcy was relieved that the flood of money being spent to outfit the building was finally starting to slow down as the bulk of the expenses were for odds and ends picked up at Home Depot or Lowes by Ron or one of his committee members. It was clear they had no clue just how much money they were spending. They probably did spend less than if they had contracted the project, but not knowing what was coming was making Darcy nervous.

A few days before they were to move, Ron held their first SLT meeting in several weeks. Ted and Bryan had seen the renovated office already because they had been enlisted to help with some of the painting to have everything done on time. It was comical that this is where Ron decided he could save money. Both Ted and Bryan were salaried, so dragging them to the office on a Saturday afternoon was essentially free. Daryl and Darcy knew that Ron wouldn't have dared asking either of them to finally help with the project after excluding them from everything up to this point.

As usual, Darcy, Daryl, Ted, Bryan, and Shirley all showed up before Ron.

"You guys should see the place," said Ted enthusiastically. "I have to hand it to Ron; he's done a great job."

"I should hope so," said Darcy. "It certainly has cost enough. So much for being frugal."

"Oh, I think he was frugal," said Bryan. "He found a couple of idiots to be his slave labor," nudging Ted.

"You could have said no, Bryan," said Shirley.

Bryan gave her a hard look, "Are you kidding me?"

They all laughed as Ron walked into the room. "What did I miss?"

"Oh, Shirley just made a stupid joke," said Bryan.

For the next hour, Ted talked about the new building and how the move would go. "I have comprised a list of people who will be involved in the move on Saturday. Everyone else needs to stay away. They'll just be in the way."

"But Ron," said Darcy, "I've had a couple of managers ask me if they could come in and set up their offices. Next week is month-end, and we are going to be busy."

"Then they can wait until next weekend," he answered. "Their computers and phones will be hooked up and operational on Monday when they come in. That's all they'll need."

Darcy just shook her head and let it go. She knew Betty was not going to be happy, but Darcy knew she wasn't going to win this battle.

"Oh, and another thing, evening access to the building will be very limited next week because of the security system," said Ron.

At that Darcy knew she had to weigh in. "Ron, did I mention that next week is month-end? My department routinely works late hours on the last day of the month. If you knew access to the building was going to be limited this week, why in the world did you schedule the move for this weekend? You were so adamant that our group not get pulled into this move because we had a business to run, yet this is going to be a big hindrance upon running the business."

"Okay Darcy, I'm sorry," Ron said. "I didn't think about how it would affect your department's work."

Daryl jumped in to give Darcy support. "That's why we should have been kept in the loop, Ron. What happened to the budget we were all going to see and approve? Listen, I'm sure everything looks great, and it's going to be a wonderful place to take our clients, but the way this thing was done was just wrong. Don't you think the rest of us would have liked to have some input?"

Ron was speechless for several seconds. He had no clue that he had done anything wrong; he had worked so hard to make the place perfect. "I'm sorry to all of you," said Ron. "None of this ever occurred to me. I was just so busy working on getting it ready."

"Listen, Ron," said Darcy. "We aren't here to beat up on you. What's done is done. But we need to figure out what we are going to do about next week. I can tell you that not only are my managers not going to be happy working all week in an office they don't have time to move into, but they are going to find the restricted working hours unacceptable."

"Okay," Ron said quickly, "we'll need to designate an IT person to stay until the last person leaves each day. Can you take care of that Daryl? If any of your managers want to come on Sunday afternoon, I'll arrange to have someone here to accommodate for a couple of hours. Please just let me know as soon as possible."

"Okay, I'll see if anyone is interested," said Darcy, "thanks, Ron." One thing she knew for sure: she surely wouldn't be one of the people in the office on Sunday afternoon. She'd work amongst unopened boxes until she could get access to the building in the afternoon, after hours.

The following Monday, Darcy showed up at the office at eight o'clock sharp. As she walked through, she was amazed at Ron's decorating ability—the place was beautiful. Smiling to herself, she thought how he had picked the wrong profession. While making her way to her new office, she passed Betty sitting in her immaculate, professionally decorated office.

"Wow, you were busy yesterday," Darcy said as she popped her head into Betty's office. "You even hung all of your pictures. I'm impressed."

"Yes, I normally wouldn't have come to the office on a Sunday, but I couldn't fathom having unopened boxes in my office all week. Sam was hovering outside my office all afternoon." Sam was the IT guy that Daryl had designated to be the last in the building all week.

"Well, Sam was being paid, so don't feel too sorry for him," said Darcy. "It looks great, Betty." She loved that she was located close to Betty and the admin department. At the other office, she was on the opposite side of the building.

When Darcy walked into her own office, she just groaned. There were boxes everywhere. She stepped over a few to get to her desk. When she opened her email, the first one she read was from Ron to the entire Charlotte staff. It read, "I hope everyone enjoys our beautiful new building. Please be sure to have yourself unpacked by next Monday morning as we want to be able to start scheduling customer visits."

Darcy rolled her eyes and thought, *How the hell am I going to get that done?* She had plans to be out of town the following weekend, and she didn't want to impose too much on poor Sam this week. Just then, Bob walked into her office. She was clearly surprised to see him.

"What are you doing here?" she asked Bob.

"I wanted to see the new digs," he said. "You guys did a great job. Thanks."

"Don't thank me," Darcy responded. "It was all Ron." She knew Bob already knew it. Ron had a knack for taking credit when credit was due. "I just pay the bills."

"Well, I'm amazed at how he accomplished all this on such a tight budget," said Bob. Darcy was almost speechless.

"What tight budget are you speaking of Bob?" she asked.

"Ron told me it was going to come in under $50,000," said Bob.

"Well Bob, I think you might have gotten some wrong information. I have Ben and Jake compiling the numbers, and it's going to be much more than $50,000." Bob looked at her with a blank stare.

"How much?" he asked.

"I don't know yet, Bob. The expenses are still being accounted for. A lot is coming through on expense reports, so I can't be sure we have everything. We still don't have invoices from your handymen either." Bob's confusion turned into annoyance.

"Why do you suppose Ron would give me a number so low?" asked Bob.

"In his defense, Bob," said Darcy, "he had no idea how much was being spent. The other managers and I pushed to do a budget and have everything approved through the management team; Ron insisted that we stay out of it. You have to admit, though, he did a great job." Bob saw no humor in her statement. He mumbled something under his breath and left.

The next morning, Ron called Darcy into his office. Before she could sit down, he asked her, "Darcy, what were you thinking telling Bob that the move cost so much?"

"Well, Ron," she answered, "I couldn't lie to him. He somehow got the impression that this project was going to cost less than $50,000."

"He got that impression because that's what I told him," said Ron. "There's no way it cost more than that."

"With all due respect, Ron, we've been tracking the expenses: You must count all the trips to Lowes and Home Depot, in addition to the electrical and furniture. We've also got the cost of Bob's handymen, for which I've yet to see an invoice. We aren't even tracking the overtime that was involved, either."

"How come I wasn't told that you were tracking the expenses?" asked Ron.

Darcy gave him a puzzled look. "Are you kidding? That happens to be my job. I asked Ben and Jake to start tracking from the beginning for tax purposes. Shirley has been giving us your expenses. I'm going to refrain from asking why you insist on using your personal credit card when you've been carrying around a company card with a $10,000 limit for years."

"I don't like your tone," Ron said. "Just what are you implying?"

"I'm not implying anything, Ron. Just curious."

"You listen to me, Darcy," said Ron with contempt. "Don't you ever blindside me like that again."

Darcy stood and turned to exit Ron's office. "Now I guess you know how it feels."

She passed Shirley's office as she left. Shirley glanced at her with a frightened look. Darcy had no doubt Shirley would bear the brunt of Ron's anger because of the help she had given to her. Darcy felt a pang of guilt and mouthed the words, "I'm sorry," to Shirley.

# ENOUGH IS ENOUGH

**For several weeks, Ron and Darcy's** working relationship was more strained than ever. How could he be mad at her for doing her job? She didn't intentionally blindside him. If he had been honest with Bob, this would not have happened. Darcy began to wonder if Bob was finally beginning to question Ron's job performance. He had always ignored the constant barrage of red flags, from the increasingly poor financial performance to the occasional letter he would get from a disgruntled ex-employee. Plus, he'd recently started to call Darcy more often with questions about the financials, and he was coming into the office more often, which always made Ron nervous.

One day, to Darcy's surprise, Ron walked into her office, closed the door, and said, "Darcy, I need you to do me a favor. You and Sue seem to have a good working relationship." Darcy nodded her head.

Sue Stephens was the Director of the Human Resources department. She was three or four years from retirement and had a wealth of knowledge about everything from compliance to recruiting. Burgess was lucky to have someone with Sue's level of experience. The only problem was Ron hated it when Sue would disagree with him on how to handle employee issues. Ron had a habit of acting impulsively when there were problems, and Sue was always there to warn him of the implications. She was particularly annoyed with Ron when she found out about his secret communications with Daryl a few years earlier as she wasn't told about Daryl until after Ron had made him an offer. Sue was sure if she had the opportunity to review Daryl's non-compete, they could have saved a lot of money in legal bills. Over the years, Ron's actions had cost the company a great deal in legal expenses. Much of which would have been avoided had he listened to Sue. Because of this, Sue and he were at odds most of the time.

"Sure, Sue and I get along well," she responded. "Why do you ask?"

"I'll be honest, Darcy," he answered. "She's driving me up the wall. She fights me at every turn. I was wondering if we could just start having her report to you." Darcy was a little shocked at this. She had always thought that Human Resources should fall under her realm, but Ron wanted to be able to have total control over personnel issues. This was certainly a surprising turn of events.

"Sure Ron, I'd be happy to take over," she said. "Does Sue know about this?" Darcy wasn't sure how Sue would take it. It was a little different reporting to the CFO than reporting to the president. "No, I haven't told her," he answered. "I was hoping you could do it."

"Okay. Any idea what I should say when she asked me why?"

"Just tell her it's because she works so closely with payroll," he answered. "It just makes sense."

The next day Darcy went to see Sue in her office. "How are you, Sue?" she asked.

"Great," Sue answered, "I really love the new office. I've got to hand it to Ron; he really did a great job."

"Yes, he sure did," said Darcy.

"Speaking of Ron, he and I were talking yesterday about department structure. We were thinking that it might be more efficient if you became part of my team; we usually end up calling you into the staff meetings anyway because we have so many questions for you. Now you'll be a permanent fixture."

Sue just stared at Darcy with a blank look on her face. "Be honest with me Darcy," she said. "What the hell brought this on? This has 'Ron' written all over it. Right down to the fact that he had you break the news to me. I know he's pissed at me most of the time, but I just want to do my job, Darcy. And it's my job to warn about compliance issues. If I try to tell him something he doesn't want to hear, he tells me I'm being antagonistic. I refuse to be another Ted or Bryan and kowtow to Ron's every whim." Darcy sat calmly and let Sue vent her frustration.

"Listen, Sue," Darcy said, "I'm not going to sit here and try to mislead you about this. Ron was the one who brought this up. But, to tell you the truth, Sue, it's always been my opinion that HR should be part of the accounting and admin teams. You and I work well together, and you'll have an advocate when Ron needs to be reined in. I can also act as your buffer. I'm pretty good at that—just ask Betty."

Sue laughed and said, "Maybe that wouldn't be so bad."

As year-end approached, it was clear that for the first time in a long time there would be a decline in overall sales from the previous year. Very few salespeople met their quotas. In fact, the only ones who did were the account reps in the major markets who barely had to lift a finger to exceed quota. In addition to meeting quota, to qualify for President's Club, the account reps were required to bring in five qualified referrals to the Managed Services division. Not one of the reps who met quota had done that. Darcy was relieved that no one had qualified because Ron had arranged a trip to London for the President's Club. They certainly could not afford such a trip with their cash flow issues.

The final employee meeting of the year was usually the time that Ron talked about how the company had progressed throughout the year. It was at this meeting that he also announced the winners of the President's Club trip. Darcy assumed that Ron would leave out that section of the program.

As Ron closed his presentation on the unique challenges the company had endured over the past year, he then said, "And finally, I'd like to commend the six exceptional salespeople who will be travelling to London, England, in April. First, from our Greensboro branch, we have Chuck Mills and Debra Rawlings. From our Raleigh branch, we have Lori Kersey and Phil Earley. Finally, from our Charlotte office, we have Melanie Smith and Nathan Stone."

Darcy couldn't believe her ears. Only the other day, the SLT had discussed how no one had qualified for the trip. She made her way over to Daryl, who was standing in the very back of the room. "Daryl, what's going on?" she asked.

He looked at her apologetically. "Darcy, Ron came to me last night advocating for giving these guys the trip. I was adamant: 'No!' Like always, he overruled me. He said it was the managers' fault that more people had not made quota. He went on to say that he blamed the managers for not pushing the IT services component of the plan. They are the ones he is going to penalize for not meeting those benchmarks. Ron will be travelling to London with those six employees without any of the managers—including me."

Darcy was stunned. "You've got to be kidding me. Daryl, the optics on this are horrible. Our rank and file guys have been working their asses off. We have been beaten up daily about how we need to save money because sales are off. Yet, the six people in the organization who work the least hours are being escorted to London with Ron. Daryl, I know I'm preaching to the choir, but this sucks!"

"I know Darcy, I tried to talk him out of it," said Daryl. "Unfortunately, you know as well as I do that you can't tell Ron anything."

Darcy was at Ron's doorway when he returned from the meeting. She walked in behind him and closed the door. "Ron, what the hell are you doing? This looks bad to our employees. They have been hearing every day how we need to be frugal because of the revenue challenges we are facing. Now you are telling everyone that certain employees have earned a trip to Europe. I thought we had discussed at the SLT meeting the other day that no one had earned the trip."

"Darcy," Ron returned, "I understand how this must look, but we can't risk losing these salespeople. They expect this trip each year." Darcy was taken aback at Ron's honesty.

She shook her head and said, "So, you can't risk losing these six salespeople, but many employees who work their butts off get nothing? If sales were up, it would be a different story. But our sales sucked this year."

"I'm sorry Darcy," he said. "The die is cast—we can't change anything at this point. I've already committed us to this trip."

The next few months were rather uneventful. For the most part, Ron stayed out of everyone's way, but there was an absence of the energy the New Year normally brought. Everyone just seemed to go through the motions. The first quarter numbers were about the same as they had been the previous year, which meant that they were bad. About the time the numbers came out, the chosen ones in the sales department were preparing for their big trip. That did nothing to lessen the sting the first quarter numbers brought.

Late one afternoon, Bob came into Darcy's office and closed the door. "Darcy, what is going on with these numbers?"

"Oh hi, Bob, I didn't realize you were here," she said. "I'm not sure I understand what you are asking. It's obvious that sales are flat, expenses are about the same, so our first quarter was virtually identical to last year. Not much else to say."

"I don't understand why we can't get out of this rut," he wondered out loud.

"Well, Bob, in my opinion, we have several high-dollar sales-people who don't need to start working until the second quarter, and they still make great money," she answered. "My guess is, we'll start to see things pick up about a month after those guys get back from their trip." He gave her a puzzled look. Then she said, "Listen, Bob, perhaps you should be having this conversation with Daryl. Why don't you start getting some other perspectives, besides Ron's, about how things are going … again, my opinion." He gave her a blank stare and turned to leave her office. She knew that he would never go to Daryl to find out what the problems were. That's what Ron was for.

The day before the trip Darcy, Daryl, Ted, and Bryan all received an email from Ron that read:

As you know, I will be travelling next week on the President's trip. The team will be gone April 28–May 2 (two of these days are over a weekend). In the event something out of the ordinary happens while I am away, I would like you to call me. If I'm not available, you four will collectively make any decision that needs to be made. I will have international calling on my phone, plus I will be using the "WhatsApp" app to send and receive text messages. Please make sure you download that app to your phone. I will have my cell with me at all times.

Darcy could not believe what she was reading. The management team that was being left behind collectively had more than fifty years of service, and Ron didn't think he could be out of the country for three business days without them texting him on What's-fricking-App?

At that moment, Ted walked into her office and said, "I don't know about you, but I feel like I'm about sixteen, and it's the first time my parents left me at home alone."

Darcy laughed and said, "Great analogy. If Ron thinks I'm going to download that stupid app on my phone so I can 'stay connected' he's crazy. He really needs to chill out and go enjoy his trip."

The first day that Ron was gone everything was uneventful. At the end of the day, the team all met at Darcy's door.

"Congratulations you guys," Bryan said, "We made it through an entire day without ruining the company."

"I have to say, I was a little concerned with Ted being so far away," Daryl joked.

"So, did anyone WhatsApp him?" asked Darcy.

They all looked at her and said, "Hell no," in unison.

The next day, Sue came into Darcy's office and closed the door. "Darcy, we have a situation that needs attention: Lloyd Stover, one of our technicians in the eastern part of the state, has been caught harassing people on his social media, as well as making very negative comments about the company and has named specific employees in his posts. I talked to one of the attorneys at our law firm about it, and their recommendation is to terminate him immediately. It's a clear violation of the company's social media policy, and the employee handbook states that offenders will lose their jobs if the policy is abused."

"You've got to be kidding," Darcy groaned. "How incredibly stupid is that? Drinking while on social media should be outlawed."

Sue laughed and said, "My guess is if they did that, political discourse in this country would be much more congenial."

"But seriously, Sue," said Darcy. "This needs to be taken care of today."

"What about Ron?" Sue asked.

"Sue, I'm going to make an executive decision on this," said Darcy. "I don't want to run the risk of Ron telling us to wait until he gets back, because that won't be until Monday. Darcy picked up the phone to call Bryan. "Poor Bryan. It's not going to be easy to find a replacement. Lloyd is an experienced tech. His work will be missed."

Bryan stood facing Darcy as she sat at her desk. The color had drained from his face. "Darcy, how can something like this happen?" he asked. "Lloyd is one of my best techs."

"I know, Bryan, but you've seen the posts," she said. "The guy has some real issues. Do you want him having contact with our customers?"

"Of course not," Bryan said. "I know what we need to do. I just can't believe it's happening. This is going to make my life miserable for a while."

"I know, Bryan," she said. "I'm so sorry. How do you want to handle it? It really needs to be done as soon as possible."

"I'm going to call his manager, Jeff, and get him to do it today. There's no way I can make the drive and get there by the end of the work day. I'll leave first thing in the morning so I can meet with the team. There will be a lot of questions." Darcy felt terrible for Bryan. She knew that he would be doing a lot more travelling until he could get a qualified replacement for Lloyd.

On Monday morning, Darcy walked into the office knowing she needed to get the confrontation with Ron out of the way as soon as possible. She decided to give him a few minutes to get settled before she broke the news to him. She realized that she would face some stiff repercussions for the way she handled the Lloyd situation, but still felt that she did the right thing.

When Darcy started down the hall toward Ron's office, Sue came rushing her way with an angry look. "Darcy, I need to speak to you right now," she demanded.

"Okay, let's go back to my office," Darcy said with concern in her voice. When they reached her office, Darcy closed the door and turned toward Sue. "Sue, what happened?"

Sue, almost yelling, said, "Ron is what happened. He was at my office door first thing this morning. Darcy, he yelled at me for coming to you about the situation with Lloyd. He said that I should not have spoken to anyone but him about it and that he, and only he, should have made the decision to fire Lloyd. Darcy, I'm so confused. First, you guys tell me that I need to start reporting to you. Then when I come to you, my boss, with an issue, I get yelled at. I didn't say this to Ron, but I will be resigning as soon as I have a chance to put it in writing."

Darcy was as confused as Sue. "Sue," she started, "please don't do this. Let me talk to Ron and find out exactly why he reacted that way. Honestly, if I had known this would happen, I certainly would not have allowed you to come into his crosshairs. This was my decision, and he should not have taken his anger out on you.

As for the whole thing about you not coming to me: I have no idea what brought that on."

By now, Sue had calmed down and just looked at Darcy and shook her head. "Darcy, can I ask you a question?"

Darcy nodded.

"Why are you still here? I mean, I look at all of you—Ted, Daryl, and Bryan. I don't understand why you put up with the way he treats you. How many more times are you going to let him humiliate you in front of the employees? Don't try to talk me out of leaving. I was already thinking about only working another year or so anyway. I just don't want to do this anymore." Darcy realized, she didn't want to try to convince Sue to stay. Why should Sue put up with the abuse any longer?

"Okay Sue, I understand what you are saying," she started. "I promise I won't ask you to stay. Just, please, be sure before you do this. You are going to be sorely missed."

"Thank you, Darcy," said Sue. "I'm going to miss you, and almost everything about this place." She came around the desk, gave Darcy a hug, and left.

Sue left Darcy with a lot to think about. She thought that there were those who looked at her as Ron's doormat, but to hear it from Sue stung a little.

As soon as she collected herself, she again headed for Ron's office. As she reached his doorway, she heard him slam his phone down after berating Bryan for not being in the Charlotte office today. He looked up and saw Darcy approaching, and she could already tell that this was not going to be a friendly conversation. She walked in and shut the door. "Ron, what the hell did you say to Sue? She just quit."

A look of surprise flashed on his face. "If she did, Darcy, you can blame yourself," he said angrily.

"Excuse me?" she said defiantly. "I'm not the one who yelled at her for going to her boss with a situation that needed immediate attention. Where do you get off by telling one of my employees that she should have come to you, and only you?"

As if ignoring her he asked, "Darcy, why didn't you wait until I got back to deal with this, and why didn't you call me?"

"First of all, Ron," she answered, "everything that transpired was my decision alone, and you owe Sue an apology. Second, we didn't call you because we were sure that you would have told us to wait, which you just confirmed. We were advised by the attorneys to deal with it immediately."

"Who talked to the attorneys?" Ron asked. "I have made it clear to Sue on many occasions that she is not to call the attorneys without my approval."

"Ron," said Darcy trying to control her rising anger, "I don't understand why you are getting so hung up on how you were left out of the loop, and not taking into consideration what we were dealing with last week. Are you saying that if you had been here, you would not have handled it the way we did? Bryan even agreed, and you know how much grief this is causing him. Ron, believe it or not, you aren't always the smartest person in the room."

As soon as the words came out of her mouth, she wished she had not made the last statement. But she had wanted to say that to him for so long. Ron looked at her with shock on his face.

"Listen, Darcy," Ron said, "don't you ever again make a decision that big without consulting me first. I may not be the smartest person in the room, but I'm still your boss. Since the only reason I moved Human Resources to your department was because of Sue, now that she's leaving, the new person will again report to me. That way, nothing like this will ever happen again."

Darcy arose from her chair. As she headed for the door, she shook her head and said, "Whatever, Ron."

That afternoon and evening, Darcy could not get Sue's observations out of her head. Though she hated taking her work home, she decided she needed to discuss what happened with Jimmy. He could always give her an unemotional take on circumstances at work. Most of the time, he showed her how she was blowing things out of proportion. However, on this evening as she related what had happened the last few days, his reaction was quite different. "Darcy, you need to get out of there," he said. "I know you love that company, but Ron is making you miserable. I can tell how unhappy you are."

Darcy was shocked by what she had just heard him say. He was supposed to be talking her out of her need to leave, which was becoming greater by the day. "Jimmy, what are you saying?" she asked. "Do you forget we have two kids in college? What would I do?"

"We've been saving our entire careers. We have a cushion. Haven't you always wanted to own your own business? There's no better time than now to do that. If I remember right, I believe I tried my best to get you to do this five years ago." He smiled and continued, "See, if you would have just listened to me then, you would have avoided all of the bad feelings." She looked at him and finally smiled and gave him a hug. What would she do without him?

"Jimmy, I don't know how to thank you for your support. It may be tough at first, but I think—no, I know—you are right. I'm going to do it tomorrow."

As soon as Darcy reached the office the next day, she began to craft her letter of resignation. It was much more difficult than she thought it would be. There was so much she wanted to say, but knew that it would be best to keep it as professional as possible. She didn't want to burn any bridges.

After an hour of writing and re-writing, she printed a copy for Ron, and emailed a copy to Bob. She was almost relieved to see that Ron was not at his desk. She wanted him to read the letter before they spoke. As she left Ron's office, she passed Daryl in the hallway.

"Hey Darcy, I heard about Sue," he said. "What happened? Did Ron really blow up at her because of the whole Lloyd thing?"

"Yeah, he did some irreparable damage yesterday," she said and walked away.

About an hour later, Ron came rushing into her office. "What is this all about?" he asked, waving the letter in front of her.

"Well, Ron, I believe it says I quit," she said.

"Darcy, is this because of the disagreement we had yesterday?" he asked. "Maybe I overreacted. You can't do this."

Darcy looked at him and was surprised at how calm she was. "Ron, to be honest, if you had asked me this yesterday when I made the decision, I probably would have said that it had everything to do with what had just transpired. But it has very little to do with that. And, by the way, yes, I can do this. I should have done this a long time ago." About that time, her cell phone rang. The caller ID said that it was Bob. She looked up at Ron and said dismissively, "I'm sorry, Ron, but you'll have to excuse me. I really need to take this call."

When she answered, Bob's booming voice came through the phone. "Darcy, why am I reading a letter of resignation from you? What happened?"

Darcy smiled and said, "Hi Bob. I hope all is well. Yes, you are reading a letter of resignation. What happened, Bob, is that last night I came to a decision that I should have come to years ago. I can't tell you how liberating it is."

"Well, what can we do to make you change your mind?" he asked.

"Bob, I appreciate that," she answered, "but I can honestly say that there is nothing you can say or do that would change my mind. Like you said to Ron and me five years ago: I'm tired. I want to go do my own thing."

At that, Bob realized that this time Darcy had put a lot of thought into her decision, and had obviously discussed it with Jimmy. "I just don't understand," he said. "Why now? Something must have happened to bring this on. Did Ron do something?"

She laughed and said, "Bob, what got me here is the culmination of a lot of things that I have been ignoring for a long time. What I really want to say to you is thank you for the tremendous opportunity you gave me. You have been very good to my family and me. I will never forget it."

Bob was silent for a second and then said, with resignation in his voice, "No, Darcy, thank you for being a loyal friend and employee for so long. When I am in town this month, I want to sit down with you and talk more. The letter says that you will stay on for at least another month. Thanks for being flexible. We are going to have a huge hole to fill."

"Not a problem," she said. "I want to help with this transition as much as possible. I'll see you soon."

As she hung up the phone, she had a slight pang of regret. This was going to be a lot to get used to. She knew it would be impossible to walk out the door and never look back.

# MAPPING THE ROAD TO RECOVERY

**About a week after she gave** her letter of resignation, Darcy received a call from Paul Dugan, the president of Great Ridge. Paul had remained in contact with Darcy for when he had questions about the financials she had been providing. "Darcy, Bob just told me that you have resigned," he said.

"Yes, I'm sorry," she said, "I was going to give you a call before I sent Mary the new financials."

"That really puts a damper on our interest in the company," he said. "This thing was going to be difficult anyway, but now it will be a long shot."

"I'm sorry, Paul, but I just felt like it was time to leave," she said. "To be honest, I don't see how you would ever get to a number that would be acceptable to Bob."

"Darcy, I was going to call you this week, anyway," he said. "Speaking of the numbers, I'm having a lot of trouble understanding what is going on there. Up until just a few years ago, things were rolling. Now I know that the new division start-up has been a drag, but that doesn't explain the slow-down in the imaging business. I've been trying my best to find something that I can grab onto to justify paying more for this company. Can you think of anything that might have been a catalyst for this slowdown, and more importantly, is it fixable?"

"Well now, those are a couple of loaded questions," Darcy replied. "If I might make a recommendation, I think it would be a good idea to see if Bob is agreeable to bringing another member of the management team into the conversation: Daryl Hughes, who is not only the director of sales but who is also responsible for the IT services division. He agrees with me that there is some definite low hanging fruit in this company, but I think Daryl could help me better articulate what that is."

That afternoon, Paul gave Bob another call. "Bob," he said, "I'm sorry to bother you again, but I just had a conversation with Darcy. Based upon what she said to me, I think it would be valuable to have another meeting to discuss the future of the company. Darcy said a meeting that includes Daryl Hughes could be productive. She said that she and Daryl could provide some insight on what has caused the company's decline over the past few years. Do you think we could set up another meeting fairly soon?"

Bob was surprised to hear that Darcy had suggested that Daryl be part of the conversation. Ron was constantly talking about how

Daryl was a trouble maker and how the other managers didn't trust him. "If you think it would help move things forward, I'm okay with it," said Bob. "But it might be more productive if the meeting only be the four of us: you, Darcy, Daryl, and me. It might be easier for Daryl to speak freely if Ron is not in the room."

That was fine with Paul. His initial impression of Ron was not terribly positive. "Sure," he said. "And, Bob, do you think there is any way you could delay Darcy's exit? I detected some frustration that could be the reason she has suddenly decided to leave. It would be a real positive if we could come up with a way to do this and convince her to stay."

"I don't know," said Bob. "She seemed adamant this time. She did say though that she would stay and help with the transition. I guess we could slow that down."

"What do you mean by, 'this time?'" Paul asked. "Is this not the first time she has resigned?"

"To tell you the truth, Paul, it's not," answered Bob. "She tried to quit five years ago when I decided to retire and put Ron in charge. She really didn't want to work for him. They have very different management styles. I know they have had some differences over the years, but Ron says they get along fine."

"Bob, have you ever asked Darcy how she and Ron were getting along?" Paul asked.

"No," Bob answered, "I guess I haven't."

"Bob, please see if you can slow down the recruiting process for Darcy's replacement and if you could try to set up a meeting over the next couple of weeks. I'll fly down there anytime; you'll just need to give me a few days' notice."

Since Bob had plans to be in Charlotte the following week, he decided that might be a good time to have the meeting. The sooner they got everything in the open, the better. He called Daryl first to find out his availability. He knew Darcy would be available, as they already had plans to meet. "Daryl, Bob Burgess. How are you?"

Daryl was taken completely by surprise because he could not remember ever talking to Bob on the phone. "Hi, Bob, doing fine. What can I do for you?" Daryl asked, still taken aback.

"Daryl, I was hoping you could join Darcy and me in a meeting next Thursday with Paul Dugan, the president of Great Ridge Imaging. They are interested in pursuing an acquisition, and Darcy felt that it might be beneficial if you were in the meeting."

"Okay, I know about Great Ridge," said Daryl. "They've put together quite the dealership network. I can see where we would be a great strategic buy for them. How long have they been courting you, Bob?"

"It's been years, but they haven't been able to come close to my price. And it looks like the longer we wait, the further we get from that price. Apparently, Darcy told Paul that the two of you have discussed some ways to reverse this nosedive we have been experiencing the last few years. They want us so badly that they are willing to listen to some possibilities."

"Wow, this is such a surprise, Bob," said Daryl. "I mean with Darcy halfway out the door, it just sounds kind of odd."

"I know," said Bob, "it sounded strange to me also, but Paul and Darcy have stayed in close touch since they originally contacted us. He seems to think that, if we can get something going, she might be convinced to stay. Please keep this between the two of us. Darcy says she is still determined to leave once we find her replacement. I don't want her to think we have been working behind her back. Oh, and Daryl, the fact that we are meeting stays between you, Darcy, and me for the time being—we need to keep it quiet for now."

"Not a problem," said Daryl. "I sure hope Paul is right that there may be a chance to convince Darcy to stay. Ted, Bryan, and I have been miserable since she resigned. I am available next Thursday. I'll put it on my calendar. Thanks for including me."

The following Thursday, they met off-site at a local restaurant to avoid the rumor mill at the office. Darcy and Daryl had ridden together and showed up first.

"What do you want to bet that Bob is the last one here?" asked Darcy. "I don't know if he wants to make an entrance, or if he just hates being anywhere alone."

After a few minutes, Paul came in, and Darcy made the introductions. "Paul, I hope your flight wasn't too eventful. I'd like you to meet Daryl Hughes. Daryl, Paul Dugan." As they were being led to the private conference room Bob had reserved for them, he came through the door.

"Hey, everyone. Looks like I got here right on time," said Bob.

They were seated at the conference room table and the waitress came to get their lunch orders. As soon as she left, Paul began to speak.

"First, I want to thank all of you for being here today. And second, what I am doing here is a little out of the ordinary. To be perfectly honest, we should have walked on this months ago. However, as I was telling Bob the other day, something just doesn't seem right. There was a proven track record for several years, and suddenly it all stopped. Darcy, you said you thought Daryl and you together could give us an idea of what has happened, and whether or not it can be fixed."

Darcy spoke up and said, "Yes, Paul. Daryl and I have had conversations on how things can be improved operationally. However, it's my opinion that none of those things can happen as long as Ron is running the company."

At that, Bob chimed in. "Hold on. I realize we have some problems, but I don't think I'm quite ready to throw Ron overboard. He's been a loyal employee for many years."

Darcy looked at Bob and shook her head. "I was pretty sure you would say that. In fact, that's why it hasn't been brought up before this. You have a bad habit of letting anything negative about Ron that comes to your attention slide. The truth, Bob, is that he is micromanaging your company into oblivion."

At that, Daryl decided to enter the conversation. "I'm sorry Bob, but I must agree with Darcy. We are starting to lose good people because of Ron. Last Friday was Sue's last day. Darcy will be gone soon, and I have it on good authority that Bryan is trying his best to find something else."

"Yes, and I can guarantee if Ron starts treating Betty the way he treats everyone else, she will be gone by the end of the summer," said Darcy. "He's already having meetings with her and excluding me. My guess is he's started making his suggestions, which aren't really suggestions, on what to change about the admin department. It bugs the hell out of him that she has been given so much free rein. I'm telling you, Bob, if Betty leaves, you'll have a very unhappy sales department. They really don't need that right now, given all of the pressure they are under to increase the sales numbers."

"Losing Betty would be a disaster," Daryl agreed. "Everyone in sales loves her, not just because she's a great person, but because she does everything in her power to make sure they are supported by her staff."

"Okay," said Paul, "let's put aside the fact that Ron is running the company. I'd like the two of you to elaborate on the operational changes that you would make."

At that, Darcy took a folder out of her bag and pulled out a stack of papers. She gave everyone a copy. Under the title, "Proposed Operational Changes," were several bullet points:

- Immediate suspension or spin-off of the 501(c)3, Burgess Outreach—eliminating two positions.

- Re-write of complete sales commission plan with equitable territories and quotas, which rewards holding of service rates.

- Give major account reps authority to negotiate deals when necessary.

- Re-vamp Managed Services division: Renegotiate all contracts that are not our standard. Eliminate one technician. Outsource as much as possible to one of our leasing companies' Network Operations Centers (NOCs).

- Immediately begin search for mid-sized IT services firm to purchase.

- Push more authority to make decisions to middle managers. Make company less reliant on one person.

- Implement bonus plan and plan of accountability for service department.

- Re-work survey sent to customers to calculate a usable net promoter score.

- Immediately begin working on a comprehensive forecast for the coming year with input from all departments.

- Implement bonus plan for inventory clerks tied to improvement of turns. This would necessitate purchasing control at their level.

- Start closely tracking profitability at the contract level. Eliminate business that is not profitable for the company.

- Re-state company core values after getting input from all employees.

It is our contention that changes in the above procedures will immediately result in an increase in bottom line profits.

Bob read the paper slowly, and several times, while the others waited in silence. "So, the two of you came up with this?" he asked.

"Yes," answered Darcy. "Ted and Bryan also contributed. The four of us have been discussing this for quite some time."

"And you never felt you could come to me with it?" he asked.

"Right, or wrong, the answer was always 'no,' with you Bob," said Daryl. "There has never been any indication that you were willing to listen to this. Darcy told me how she had warned you about Ron several years ago. The declining numbers should have been a red flag, but you seemed to want to ignore it." Bob looked a little dejected.

"I'm so sorry, Bob," said Darcy sympathetically.

"So now what am I going to do?" Bob asked. "You've made it abundantly clear that Ron is not the person that should be running my company, and I sure as hell don't want to come back."

"May I suggest," Darcy began, with Bob nodding at her to continue, "that I think you are sitting across the table from the solution to your problem—Daryl has good experience, and I believe he would do a great job." Daryl swung his head around completely surprised at what he just heard.

"What did you just say?" Daryl asked.

"I said I think Bob should make you president of the company," said Darcy.

"What about you, Darcy?" asked Bob.

"What about me?" she said. "Nothing changes with me: I'm still leaving. However, I might be convinced to stay on indefinitely as a consultant. If you were to take our advice, and do this with the intent of eventually selling, you are going to need someone to coordinate everything that needs to be done to prepare the company. My suggestion would be to hire a strong controller to run the accounting department and promote Betty to Vice President of Admin. Put her on the team of upper managers. I would be happy to serve as your part-time strategic CFO, if I am able to bring value to the company. Which means: my offer is only good if Ron goes."

Paul sat back in his chair and smiled. This could not have turned out better. He was already thinking of ways he could use Darcy on a few of the other acquisitions he had targeted. He wondered what it would take to get Darcy to work for Great Ridge as a consultant. But that was a conversation for another day.

"Well, you guys have certainly given me a lot to chew on," Bob said. "This isn't going to be easy, but I'm starting to see that I have no choice but to do something. Daryl, you and I should meet for breakfast tomorrow. I'll send you an email with the details. Darcy, will you be in the office tomorrow?" She nodded. "Okay, keep your afternoon open. We will need to talk." He then turned to Paul. "Paul, thank you for putting together this little pow-wow … I think. My guess is we will have something to talk about sometime in the future, depending on how long it takes to right this ship."

"I'm a patient man, Bob," said Paul. "I also go after what I want. We'll stay in touch."

The next morning, Daryl and Bob met at a small restaurant a few miles from the office. Daryl did not know what to expect. It was a good sign that Bob had asked to meet him, but he gave no indication whether he was planning to offer him the presidency or fire him. Daryl sat quietly wanting Bob to drive the conversation.

"Daryl, I've had a lot to think about the last several hours. I'll admit I have had some concerns for quite a while, but I guess I just needed you and Darcy to hit me over the head with it yesterday. Everything you said made a lot of sense, but what you are asking me to do will be very difficult for me. Ron and I have been working together for thirty years; he's one of the most loyal employees I've ever had. I just can't figure out how to do this."

Daryl waited to see if Bob had finished his thought. He then said, "Bob, I completely understand how hard it will be. But I need to ask you: what about the almost twenty years that Darcy has given you, and the more than ten years both Sue and Bryan have given you? They, too, are loyal employees. Trust me, Bob: Darcy and I would not have suggested this unless we were sure it was necessary. You are going to continue to lose good people." Bob was silent for what seemed to Daryl to be an eternity.

"Okay, Daryl," said Bob. "I didn't ask you yesterday. Are you even interested in this job Darcy recommended you for?"

"Yes, Bob, I am," Daryl said. "But I really hope that you will accept Darcy's offer to be your consultant."

"No worries," said Bob, "I fully intend to do that." They spent the rest of their time discussing compensation and timing.

That afternoon, Bob showed up at the office and headed straight to Darcy. He walked in and closed the door.

"Have you talked to Daryl?" he asked.

"No, I haven't seen him," she responded.

"Well, I'm going to do it. On Friday afternoon, Daryl will be our new President. I decided to wait until Friday in deference to Ron. On Monday morning, I want you to start a search for a controller. Once we have someone on board, we'll talk about your contract. Any questions?"

Darcy couldn't believe what she was hearing. He was really going to do it. "Okay, Bob," she said.

Before Friday, Bob made a call to both Ted and Bryan to give them a heads-up before everything went down. Both were surprised, but by no means upset. Bob told them that Daryl would be calling a meeting of the upper managers early the next week to plan their course.

On Friday afternoon, Bob found Ron in his office beginning to pack up to go home for the weekend. "Hi Ron," he started. "Listen, I need to talk to you for a few minutes. I've been increasingly concerned about the health of the company. We just don't seem to be going anywhere. Despite report after report from you that things are starting to turn around in both the network services and imaging departments, we continue to be stuck. Now we have key employees starting to leave us. Ron, I've decided we need to make a change. Effective immediately, Daryl will be the new president of the company. I have put together a nice severance package for you; I hope you will think it is fair."

Ron was speechless for a moment. "Bob, I don't understand. I told you we were turning the corner. I don't think I can be blamed for Darcy and Sue leaving. Darcy seriously dropped the ball while I was in London, and poor Sue got caught up in the misunderstanding. If Darcy had done what she was instructed to do when I left, none of this would have happened. Her inability to take my direction on anything was beginning to hurt the company. If I can get my own person in that number two position, it will make a big difference, I promise."

"I'm sorry, Ron, I've made my decision," Bob said. "Listen, one of the first items on Daryl's list is to discontinue supporting the 501(c)3. It's just too much of a burden on a company our size. If you would like to take that over, I would be happy to let you continue your work using my name. The company would only be able to minimally support you, but I have a small office in a strip mall that I own downtown. It's available, and I could offer it to you. I would give it to you rent-free as a donation. We won't be keeping Janet and Charles, so you can decide if you would like to take them with you."

Ron had a surprised look on his face. "You're abandoning Burgess Outreach?" he asked. "We're doing such great work."

"I know," said Bob. "You guys have built a great charity. That's why I'm making this offer. We just don't have the bandwidth to support it here. Ron, with the severance I am offering, it should give you time to figure out if you want to grow Burgess Outreach or do something else. That's completely up to you."

Bob stuck around the rest of the evening while Ron cleared as much as he could out of his office. There had been a big purge when they moved into the building, so it wasn't as difficult as it could have been. By the time Ron left, Bob was close to being physically ill—this was one of the most painful things he had ever done.

A few minutes before Bob went to Ron's office on Friday, he sent an email to the entire company calling a meeting for Monday morning. The employees in Charlotte would meet in the warehouse, and the meeting would be transmitted by video to the other offices. Everyone was encouraged to attend. Rumors ran rampant throughout the company the rest of the afternoon. The consensus was that Bob would be announcing that he was selling the company. Many said they would be taking the weekend to dust off their résumés.

On Monday morning, Darcy took her position behind all the employees seated in the warehouse in anticipation of Bob's big announcement. Ron's absence was causing a buzz. Once everyone had settled and the video feeds to the branches had been established, Bob began.

"So, I guess all of you are wondering why I called you here today. Well, the truth is, I wasn't sure if some of you even knew who I was." The audience began to laugh. "I'm looking at all these young faces, and I'm beginning to think some of you were in diapers the last time I held one of these meetings." Another laugh from the group. The nervousness that had hung in the air a few minutes earlier was now gone. Bob had a knack for putting people at ease. "But seriously, we've decided to make a few changes here at Burgess. First, Ron Marchetti has left the company, and will be pursuing other opportunities." There was an audible gasp from almost everyone in the room. The secret had been well-kept over the weekend. "Second, I am pleased to announce that Daryl Hughes has agreed to step into the role of President." The group immediately started to clap. Darcy could see several people turn to others at their tables and nodded their heads in the affirmative. "Third, I'm very happy to announce that Darcy Holtzman has agreed to remain indefinitely as a part-time consultant. At that, Betty swung around in her chair and gave Darcy a big smile. "Are there any questions before I turn the meeting over to Daryl?"

Someone spoke up from the crowd, "So you aren't selling the company?"

Bob flashed a big smile and said, "Is that what you all thought?" Several people in the audience nodded their heads. "Come to think of it, I guess you could get that idea. Sorry about that. And no, I'm not quite ready to go, yet."

At that, Daryl made his way to the front of the room, shook hands with Bob, and began. "Thanks, Bob. I can't tell all of you how excited I am for the future of our company. Bob, Darcy, and I had a great meeting last week to talk about some immediate changes we will be making. We will be having a management meeting this afternoon to plan our course. Once that is done, we will communicate that course to all of you. Thoughts any of you have regarding our future are welcomed at any time."

After a few housekeeping announcements, the meeting was adjourned. Bob followed Daryl to his new office and closed the door.

"Daryl, I wanted to let you know that Ron is going to take me up on my offer to take control of Burgess Outreach. I know you wanted to deal with that and the two related employees immediately. He didn't say whether he was going to be able to give them paid positions, but asked that we direct both to him once they are let go. Don't worry, I told him that any help we would be able to give would be minimal."

"That's fantastic," said Daryl. "The work they have been doing has been great. Maybe, one day, if we grow this thing enough, we can re-establish a stronger relationship."

That afternoon, Daryl, Darcy, Ted, Bryan, and Shirley met in the conference room. It had been an exhilarating day for all of them. The feedback that had been expressed to all of them was overwhelmingly positive.

When they were all seated, Daryl began, "Guys, let's not let this energy we are feeling today go to waste. I want to go over the items that Darcy, Bob, and I discussed the other day, and then I want your input; I really want this to be a team effort. First, we are going to stop actively supporting Burgess Outreach. I talked to Bob earlier, and Ron has agreed to take control of it so they can continue their work.

Our involvement will be offering sponsorships when we can afford, and, of course, our employees can feel free to continue to volunteer their time."

At that Ted spoke up. "Daryl, what about Janet and Charles?"

"Good question," answered Daryl. "I'm afraid we won't be able to retain them. We just don't have anything for them. Ron has asked that we have them contact him. I'm not sure if he will be able to offer paid positions to them, though. Anything else, regarding the charity?" They all shook their heads. "Okay then. Second, we will begin to re-write the sales commission plans immediately. I'd like to call a meeting of all the sales managers to help write the plan and determine territories. I'd like all of you to be at that meeting." They all nodded in agreement. "In conjunction with that, we would like to give the major account reps the authority to make some decisions when in the middle of tough negotiations against our major competitors and vendors. I want to promote Elaine to my old position and make her a part of this group. We can work with her on how much leeway we should give those guys.

Next, I think we can all agree that there needs to be some drastic change in the Managed Services division. I plan to expand Jason Miller's duties from virtual chief information officer (vCIO) to department head. He, too, should become a member of this group. We will need to work with him to standardize all the contracts, which will entail renegotiation on some. Until we can find an existing Managed Services company to buy, we need to outsource everything to one of our leasing company's network operations centers. That way we will look much bigger than we are."

At that Bryan spoke up. "Daryl, what are the plans for the tech in that department—Troy, specifically? It sounds like he might not be as busy, at least for a while. We've been swamped at the imaging help desk, and he's been helping when he can. I could sure use him full-time, because Jennifer Cox just told me the other day she wants to go back to school and will be leaving us at the end of the month."

"That's perfect," said Daryl, "because we were talking about reducing the headcount, but Troy is a good employee. I'd love to see you pick him up." Everyone around the table smiled and nodded. They loved how this was going so far.

Daryl continued, "The next thing we discussed was something of a cultural change. As I mentioned about wanting to give more authority to the more experienced reps to make some decisions, we want to encourage our middle managers to make decisions on how to run their departments. For too long we have relied on one person for the operation of this company. We need to develop young managers to have the confidence to do what they feel is right for their department. They won't always be right, but who in this room has never made a bad decision?" Everyone looked around and nodded.

"Okay, we're on a roll now. Bryan." Bryan's head popped up, coming to attention. "I know you have for a long time wanted to implement a bonus/accountability plan for the technicians."

"Yes, sir," Bryan said. "I sure have."

"Well that is going to be one of our first orders of business," said Daryl. "Oh, and don't ever call me, sir, again." He smiled. "I'm not my dad. While we are on the service department, this group needs to look at our satisfaction survey that is going out to our customers. We need to have a good tracking on the likelihood that our customers are recommending us, so we can come up with an accurate net promoter score."

"Next, I'll turn to Darcy. Starting now, we need to come up with an effective way to budget and forecast our operations. We have never taken the time to do that, and we need everyone's input. That is the first thing Darcy will be doing in her capacity as our outsourced CFO."

Bryan looked at Darcy smiled and said, "Yay, Darcy."

"Ted," said Daryl, "you know your incentive plan for the inventory clerks?" Ted nodded. "Well, I've gotten a promise from Bob that he will stop being our purchasing manager. Let's try again with that plan and get our turns to where they should be. A couple of things in Admin: First, we are going to start looking closely at contract profitability. This group is going to decide when we should fire bad customers, or even bad segments of business. If we aren't making money on a contract, then we need to have a good reason why we should keep the business. Second, I will be meeting with Betty this afternoon to promote her to Vice President of Admin. She will become a part of this group." At that everyone in the room clapped their hands.

"The last item that Bob, Darcy, and I discussed the other day was the core values of this company. The three of us decided that determining those values should be up to all employees. We are going to solicit ideas and observations from our employees on what they think makes our company special. Once we have done that, I want to create a committee with representatives from all departments to take those suggestions and come up with our true core values. Some may be the same, some may be different. This needs to be something that comes from our employees, though. Okay, guys, I'm done. Please give me your thoughts."

After a moment of silence, Ted began to clap his hands. Following his lead, Darcy, Shirley, and Bryan joined in.

Daryl's first order of business was to talk to Janet and Charles. This was the one thing that he had been dreading, so he decided to just get it done. He felt especially bad for Janet, because Burgess

Outreach had given her the ability to experience her dream job. She was devastated by the news, but he sensed that she was not terribly surprised. Everyone knew that changes were on the horizon. She had felt for some time that others at the company did not share the passion for the mission that she and Ron had. He told her to be sure to contact Ron, that perhaps they could work out an arrangement that would allow her to continue. She thanked him and left.

His meeting with Charles was less emotional. Charles had been in sales for many years and had lost more than one job during his career.

"Daryl," he said, "I wish you the best of luck. I'll be honest: I was having trouble trying to figure out just what Ron was trying to accomplish with this outreach. It's been a massive resource suck. I didn't question him, because, hell, it was paying the bills. There were no illusions that it would last forever."

"So, Charles," said Daryl, "we may have some sales spots opening in the next few months. Any interest?"

Charles thought for a minute. "I don't think so, Daryl. I think I'm sick of this industry. Give me a call in a few months, and I'll let you know if I change my mind."

"Will do," said Daryl. "Good luck to you, Charles."

After Charles left his office, Daryl decided to do one of the easy things on his list. He picked up his phone and called Betty. "Hey Betty, do you have a few minutes? I'll come to you."

"Sure Daryl," she said. "I'll be here." When he entered her office and closed the door, she looked at him nervously and asked, "Is everything okay, Daryl?"

"Absolutely," he said. "I wanted to talk to you a bit about the changes that are going on around here."

"Well, I have to say that I was relieved to hear that Darcy will be staying around, even if it is only part-time," she said. "Her leaving had me really bummed."

"Most of us felt that way, Betty," he said. "What we are going to do going forward is kind of split Darcy's job. Instead of hiring a CFO, we are going to hire a controller to handle all day-to-day duties. Darcy will continue to handle the strategic parts of her job, such as budgeting and planning. However, what we will still need is a strong manager to represent accounting and admin on our upper management team. Betty, I'd very much like to make you our Vice President of Admin and have the accounting, admin, and human resources departments report to you." Betty just stared at him. This was the last thing she expected when he asked to meet with her.

"Dang," she finally said. "I thought you were coming here to fire me or something."

"My god, Betty, why the heck would I do that?" he asked. "The whole sales department would throw me out on my ass if I did that."

"Really?" she asked. "I always got the impression from Ron that I was doing something wrong."

He laughed and said, "Betty, I think Ron may have felt a little threatened by you because you were so successful at managing your department. He wanted to be the one who fixed everything. That's commendable, but it isn't the best way to run a company. So, are you interested?"

She smiled and said, "Of course I am. This is going to be great!"

Next stop, Elaine. On his way back, Ron popped his head into her office. "Hey Elaine, what's up?" he asked.

She looked up and smiled. "You dog!" she yelled. "Why didn't you tell me?" She walked around her desk and gave him a hug. "Daryl, I'm so excited for you ... and the company. I'll be honest: I have been seriously thinking about leaving recently. The pay has been great, but everything else pretty much sucks."

"I hear you," Daryl said. "Elaine, do you have a minute to talk about some of the changes we are making?"

"Sure, Mr. President. Have a seat," she answered.

He smiled and said, "Elaine, first, effective immediately: the major account reps can do as much negotiating as you feel comfortable with. I'm leaving that completely up to you. Second, I would like you to take over as Vice President of Sales. We need your presence on the upper management team." For the first time Daryl could ever remember, Elaine was speechless. "Elaine, I need your thoughts."

"Okay," she said. "Wow! Daryl, I promise you, the sky is the limit. For so long, I have wanted to unleash this sales department. I truly believe within weeks we will be able to turn this thing around. I have dreamed about this opportunity, Daryl. Thank you so much. I will not let you down."

"Okay," said Daryl. "I thought you would be happy, but your enthusiasm is overwhelming. I think Betty put it best: this is going to be great!"

"Betty? What's up with Betty?" she asked.

"I just made her Vice President of Admin," said Daryl.

"Yes! This *is* going to be great," said Elaine.

As Daryl returned to his office, he thought about how much had been accomplished in one day. He knew that Elaine would immediately energize the sales department, and, as she said, the sky was the limit. Tomorrow he would dive into the IT services business. This would make or break him. What needed to happen would be to almost completely start over. Jason had done a great job as vCIO, but they were not getting any traction with new customers. He planned to meet with Jason and Darcy the next day to task both with targeting possible companies to acquire. Darcy had been on the front lines of several acquisitions they had made since she joined the company eighteen years earlier; she would be an integral part of this transaction.

That evening, he wrote an email to all the employees in the company announcing the changes that had been made on his first day. He again welcomed any employee to contact him directly with their comments and suggestions. The last line of the email simply read, 'More to come.'" When he got the opportunity to check his email, it was flooded with comments from the employees—almost all positive (you can't please everyone).

The next morning, he and Darcy met with Jason. When they were all settled in Daryl's office, he began.

"Jason, you and I have spoken on several occasions about the changes that need to be made in your department to ultimately be successful. So, since I finally have the authority to task you with getting those changes done, I'd like you to become our Vice President of IT Services and a part of our upper management team. Bryan has agreed to absorb Troy in his department, since once you get all the contracts either standardized or cancelled, his work will be reduced considerably. My guess is that we will initially see a decrease in revenue, but we should be able to stabilize the bottom-line losses. I'd like you and Darcy to immediately start the search for a company to purchase; I'm sure you run into competition that might be a good fit for our company. If we can buy someone who is doing this success-fully, it would bring a much-needed boost to your division."

Jason couldn't believe what he was hearing. He had been frus-trated that they were having so much trouble becoming a player in the market. When they started out, Ron had assumed that their affiliation with Burgess Industries would be immediate credibility.

But, because of some poor decisions early on, their reputation in the market still wasn't established. They didn't have a bad reputation; they just didn't have any reputation at all. When Daryl mentioned an acquisition, several competitors came to mind. He looked at Daryl and said, "Geez, Daryl, you sure do know how to take someone by surprise. I thought you were coming in here to tell me that we were scrapping the department. I can't say I would have blamed you, either. We've really been stinking it up. I truly believe we can turn this around. I know of a couple of people who would probably be interested in an acquisition. I don't know how to thank you for the opportunity. I promise I won't let you down."

He then turned to Darcy and said, "How do you want to handle this acquisition search, Darcy? I have a few ideas. It's my opinion that we put this on a fast track. I will start today on getting our current contracts fixed, but we aren't going to see anything big until we get the acquisition done."

They all agreed. Darcy and Jason set up some time to discuss companies to target and strategies for going after them.

Later that week, Daryl called a meeting with the upper management team as well as the middle managers. As they assembled in the training room, they all wondered what this could be about. The middle managers had never been asked to participate in any of the management meetings.

Daryl began the meeting by telling all the managers how important they were to the success of the company. He then said, "We need to see you guys on the front-line start taking more ownership of the workings of your departments. Let's take Clint as an example. Clint, I apologize for putting you on the spot." His choice of Clint was not random. He hoped he would make Clint realize that he needed to make some changes as soon as possible. He continued,

"So, Clint comes across a problem that is hurting the efficiency of his department. From now on, Clint should not be going to Ted with the problem. He should go to Ted with the solution. If it's a simple solution that can be implemented immediately, it should have been done by the time he gets to Ted. Don't look at this as a negative. We are empowering you to do what needs to be done to make your departments run as efficiently as possible. We will be including this group in our upper management meetings once a month, so you can report to the group your successes and your failures. Failures will be looked at as learning experiences, not circumstances to be looked upon negatively. Inaction is much worse than failure. I once had a manager tell me: it's better to apologize to your manager for something you do than to apologize for something you did not do." Clint's reaction was a definite look of nervousness. Everyone else seemed to welcome the news.

After the meeting, Darcy gestured to Bryan. She pulled him aside and asked, "Bryan, do you have a few minutes? There's something I'd like to talk to you about."

"Sure, Darcy," he said. "Lead the way." When they got back to her office, she looked at him and said, "Bryan, I need to ask you about these rumors I'm hearing. Are you looking for another job? If so, I really hope you are rethinking it. Daryl needs you right now."

He stared at her with a puzzled look on his face. "I can't believe I'm hearing this," he said. "Coming from you of all people. These changes didn't compel you to change your mind. You know as well as I do that Daryl would tear up your letter of resignation in a minute. How can you sit there and try to convince me to stay when you are jumping ship?"

"Listen, Bryan," she said, "my situation is completely different. This is something I should have done years ago, even before Bob left.

I had allowed myself to become lazy and irrelevant. This job has quite literally sucked the life out of me. I've now been given an opportunity to have the best of both worlds—I get to continue to work with you guys, but I can also test the waters with other opportunities. Bryan, you are the future of this company. I know it's a new way of thinking around here, but Daryl is a forward thinker. He's told me he wants to groom you to take on a larger leadership role. I won't speculate what that is; that's between the two of you. But, he sees leadership qualities in you that can't be taught. I just don't want you to run away from this opportunity because of things that have happened in the past."

"I don't know, Darcy," he said. "I like what I am seeing, but do you really think Daryl can turn things around?"

"Yes, Bryan, I do," she answered. "In fact, I recommended Daryl to take over after Bob finally made the decision that Ron had to go."

"Really? he asked. "I didn't think that Bob was even communicating with you."

"Yeah," she said, "he wasn't, but within the past few months he started to finally realize that things weren't getting any better, and he started asking questions. So, Daryl and I used the opportunity to stage an intervention. It worked. Daryl was as surprised as Bob that I recommended him, but I honestly think he is the most qualified to do the job."

Bryan was silent for a moment and said, "Okay, Darcy. I was scheduled to go on an interview with a large dealership in South Carolina next week. They seem really interested in me for their VP of Service job. I am going to pass on it, because I'm afraid if I get down there and they start schmoozing me, I won't come back."

She laughed and said, "You always were a sucker for schmoozing."

There were two items on the agenda at the following week's upper management meeting. They had invited all the sales managers to address the broken commission plan. Everyone realized they needed to prepare themselves for some defections once the new plans were put into effect. For that reason, Daryl and Elaine had already put out feelers for some good reps they could bring on board. They also wanted to go ahead and draft an email to the employees regarding the company core values. Daryl wanted to be sure that their effort was completely transparent. He wanted everyone to know that this was a company-wide effort.

The following week's meeting started with welcoming the regional sales managers. They began by looking at the current plan, and it was quickly obvious to even the managers with no sales backgrounds that the plan favored some and hurt others. Each of the regional managers was given an opportunity to speak about how the plan affected their sales efforts. Each spoke of underworked metropolitan areas and high turnover in the less populated areas.

Ralph Winston, from the Raleigh/Durham area, said, "Daryl, if we could be given the data on our customer base and MIF (machines in field), I think all of us could do a better job of equitably assigning accounts. That's something that we've never been trusted with. It's very hard to do an effective job managing a sales team when you don't have any leeway on commissions. We should come up with account assignments that will at least give the guys outside of the urban areas a chance at making a living. Those guys should also be given a ramp-up in pay to give them a chance to get established. Bottom line: you guys worry about the percentages and accelerators based upon our forecasts, and let us set the quotas each year. Quotas should not be stagnant. They should be based upon each rep's projected renewals in the upcoming year, plus what we expect in new business. Of course, once each of our regions are rolled up, we should meet your overall expectations for us. If we are effective with this, it should be a multi-step process; not a decree from the powers that be."

They all agreed that the first step would be to let each regional manager look at their account bases and determine what they could expect to do in renewal business and new business. Each would send their budgets to Elaine, who would look at everything in total to come up with the overall sales budget to present to the upper management team. They would determine if the numbers from each region looked reasonable and in line with expectations for the coming year. They would then come up with the accelerators for over-achievement, which would be paid in the form of a quarterly bonus. There would also be a punitive part of the plan for not maintaining service rates for contracts on the sold equipment or the minimum gross profit for each deal. This would come by way of a reduction in the percentage commission paid.

They realized that they were over six months from the start of a new fiscal year, and agreed that they would try to put together a six-month forecast using the new process so they could try to implement something immediately. There would need to be some concessions made, but they all felt that something could be done in the short term.

Once they agreed on the outline, the regional managers were sent to begin working on their individual six-month budgets.

Daryl then turned to core values. "Some of you were not in our last meeting, so I wanted to let you know that we have decided to re-think our company core values. Darcy, Ted, Bryan and I felt that there was a less-than-enthusiastic acceptance of the values we currently have posted. We have discussed how this really should be something to which everyone in the company contributes. Is there someone in this group who could volunteer to craft an email to everyone soliciting their ideas on what they each feel the core values are that make Burgess such a great company? There are those who will not choose to participate, but it's my hope that we get many serious replies. I would like this to be an email that comes from all of us, and I hope each of you will encourage participation amongst your team. Any volunteers?"

"I'll do it," said Elaine almost immediately. "I think this is a very big part of our marketing efforts. We need to be very careful to make this positive, instead of just admitting that we screwed up the first time."

"Agreed," said Ted. "Remember when we had talked about trying to get Ron to do this as part of the re-branding for the thirty-year anniversary? If we can get this turned around quickly, we could use that as our excuse."

"That's perfect," said Elaine. "I'll send each of you a draft this afternoon."

They all soon received a note from Elaine showing her proposal for the company-wide email on core values. By the end of the day, after a few minor changes, the email was sent to everyone from the entire upper management team. They asked that their responses be returned in one week. At that time, they would ask for a volunteer from each department to serve on a committee that would compile the results and come up with the company core values. That committee would then work with the marketing department on the new artwork stating the values that would be posted at all the Burgess locations.

The next day, Jason and Darcy met to discuss possible acquisition targets. Darcy began by asking Jason if he had any thoughts on who would be a good match.

After a pause, Jason answered, "A couple of people came to mind when Daryl mentioned it the other day. But I had almost forgotten about a guy that I talked to last year who would be perfect."

Darcy perked up and asked, "Who?"

"A guy named Harry McDonald," he answered. "He owns a small to mid-sized IT services company and has been in the market for twenty years. He's got a very good reputation. He approached me last year because he's looking for an exit and thought we might be interested in acquiring his company. He wants to continue working but is tired of running the business. What was interesting about it was that he said that he would be willing to negotiate a pay-out over time. It sounded good to me, so I took it to Ron. He said we couldn't afford an acquisition because the division had been such a drag on the company. He told me not to say anything to any of the other managers, because all of you were advocating shutting the division down. Ron said he was the only thing standing in the way of a shutdown, and that we shouldn't stir things up with talk of an acquisition."

Darcy shook her head and said, "Jason, we are the ones who have been pushing for an acquisition. You were right: someone who is willing to do a pay-out would be perfect. That isn't normally the best situation for a seller. He must think that with our infrastructure we could grow quickly. I'd love to talk to him. Can you set up a meeting with the three of us?"

"Sure," said Jason. "I just hope that he hasn't already partnered with someone else."

"Me, too," said Darcy.

The following week, the managers decided to concentrate on the service department.

"Bryan, can you give us an idea of what kind of accountability plan you have in mind for the technicians?" asked Daryl.

"Sure thing," he said. "We have been a member of BEI (Business Equipment Information) Services for about a year. BEI accumulates data from hundreds of dealerships just like us. We send all our data related to service to them monthly, and they compile and benchmark our performance against hundreds of other dealerships. They do these calculations down to the technician level. They also offer a comprehensive incentive program for technicians, which rates their individual productivity, efficiency, and effectiveness. It pays a commission on total copies managed in their territories. If the total cost for each managed copy is below a set goal, then part of the savings is paid back in commission. If they exceed the expected cost per managed copy, the excess is deducted from their quarterly bonus. Basically, each technician needs to concentrate on three things: (1) more calls per day, (2) make each machine work longer between calls, and (3) use only the necessary parts to fix the problem. Most dealerships see at least a 20 percent reduction in service cost when this is implemented. The downside is that there are a few technicians out there who have become lazy because there has been no accountability. Those guys are not going to be happy with the fact that we will be tracking when they start and when they finish each day. Some are our most senior technicians who, to this point, have been paid on seniority instead of merit. Honestly, we may lose a few. That's it in a nutshell. What do you guys think?"

Betty spoke up. "Bryan, why aren't we using this now?"

Bryan looked at Daryl, then Darcy.

"Correct me if I'm wrong, Bryan," stated Darcy. "I believe Ron was concerned about the loss of those senior guys."

Bryan nodded.

"Well, it seems to me that if they don't want to work, we don't want them anyway," said Betty. They all laughed.

Then Bryan said, "Yeah, that's been my frustration, Betty."

"Okay, are we all in agreement that we immediately implement the BEI technician commission plan?" asked Daryl. Everyone nodded in the affirmative.

"The next thing we need to discuss," he said, "is the question-naire that is going to our customers. Our questions are way too vague. Please chime in if you disagree. There are three things, and only three things, we should be asking to get an accurate net promoter score: First, how likely are you to recommend us to family, friends, or col-leagues, on a scale of zero to ten? Zero being not likely at all; ten being extremely likely. Second, why are you giving us this rating? Third, what can we do to make our service to you better?"

"That's really all we need, Daryl," said Elaine in agreement. "Again, I know I always seem to gravitate to marketing, but being able to advertise a high net promoter score can really help our marketing efforts."

"Any other comments?" asked Daryl.

"Sounds good," said Bryan. "I can get this updated on our ques-tionnaire today. Our software will tabulate the score based upon the first question."

"Great," said Daryl. "Betty, I know your department has been tracking profitability on the contract level. How is that going?"

"Well, I'm glad you asked," she replied. "We are getting some interesting findings." She passed around a contract profitability report for each person at the table. "It seems that there are certain models of the high-end machines that we are not pricing as we should. We are losing our shirts on every single one of them. When I brought this up a few months ago, I was told that this pricing was the only thing that kept us competitive. I still have trouble understanding why we would want to sell something that we can't make money on. I'm not saying that the entire segment is non-profitable, just a few machines."

"I think that is a reasonable question, Betty," said Elaine. "I think we have avoided addressing because we were afraid we would find that the entire segment was under-performing. Ron desperately wanted to establish us as a player in this segment. I, too, think that it is important, but since we don't get the same favorable pricing on the higher -end machines as some of our competitors, it's very difficult to show a profit. I think it's a good strategy to look at this at the machine level, and only compete with the equipment on which we can make a profit."

"Good," said Daryl. "Let's look at this every week. Betty, if you could take some time each meeting and report to us on the problem contracts. We will collectively decide on what to do. Obviously, we will need to look at this on a case-by-case basis. If we have a high-end machine placed with a high-profit customer, we may not want to do anything."

About a week after their meeting, Jason showed up in Darcy's doorway with a big smile on his face. "I did it, Darcy," he said. "I finally tracked down Harry McDonald. He wants to meet with us."

"Oh, that's great," Darcy said. "When?"

"Tomorrow," he answered. "He sounds very motivated, and didn't seem to care that I knew it."

"You can't ask for more than that," said Darcy.

The next day, Jason and Darcy met Harry at a local coffee shop. Harry was still in his fifties, but the stress of running a successful business in a very competitive environment was obviously beginning to take its toll.

"Jason, it's so good to see you again." Harry then turned to Darcy and said, "You must be Darcy. Thank you both for reaching out."

"Our pleasure," said Darcy. "It's my understanding that this meeting is long overdue. Why don't you tell me what you have in mind, Harry?"

For the next hour, Harry gave them the history of McDonald IT Services. He explained how none of his four children had any interest in continuing with the company. He then digressed into a tirade about how ungrateful young people were today and, if he had it to do over, he would not spoil his kids as he had.

Darcy smiled to herself and thought of Bob's three children, none of who wanted anything to do with Burgess Industries. Harry said he was not ready to quit working, but was sick of running the company. He liked the idea of partnering with an imaging company, because they were selling to the same people. He said the reason he had not approached another dealership in the past year was because if he did it, he wanted to go with the best. Darcy was pleasantly surprised to hear that. Even with the internal problems the past few years, Burgess had been able to retain its stellar reputation in the market. By the end of the meeting, Darcy had a signed non-disclosure agreement that she had brought, even though it was a bit presumptuous on her part. Harry agreed to send Darcy a list of items, which not only included financial reports, but also operational items such as marketing campaigns and the organizational chart.

Over the next few weeks, Darcy reviewed financials, Betty and Jason reviewed contracts, and Daryl and Elaine went through the customer list. One thing became obvious to all of them: Harry was a good businessman. If they could come to an agreement, he could help Burgess IT move to the next level. When the time came for the negotiations, Bob came to town. This is where he was in his element. To Darcy, the valuation was easy to come up with. She was glad to see that Harry had insisted his company not become product centric. A large percentage of his revenue was recurring through service contracts. Because Harry was willing to structure the sale with a payout over time, Bob's heartburn at the price was lessened a great deal. That did not stop Bob from putting on his master negotiator hat. Eventually, Bob and Harry hammered out a deal in which each thought he was getting screwed. That, in Darcy's mind, meant that it was a good deal for both. Harry stood to make a great deal of money if he could, over the next few years, help Burgess IT grow at a reasonable rate. Burgess IT was getting a needed shot in the arm for a relatively low initial payout.

# THE BIG TURNAROUND

**The responses to the core values** questionnaire started to come back. The management team was amazed that they received a 60 percent response rate, which was about 20 percent higher than expected. A committee was selected with representatives from every department to use the responses to come up with the Burgess core values. Elaine was selected to be the management representative to moderate the meetings of the committee. They were tasked to have the project completed by September, which was the month in which they would celebrate Burgess's thirtieth anniversary.

By the end of June, a forecast for the second-half of the year had been put together based upon the sales expected by the regional sales managers. The new commission plans were rolled out, with some accommodations for the reps who most benefited from the old plans.

They eased those reps into the idea that things were going to change. Over the next few months, they lost one rep in Raleigh and one in Greensboro. This was not a surprise, and Elaine had replacements within weeks. The managers were initially wary of the forecast that the regions had submitted—they felt that they were being overly aggressive. However, by year-end, they would exceed the forecast by a solid 10 percent. Confident that the changes were making a real difference, the regions turned in an overall sales budget for the next year that had a year-to-year increase of 17 percent. This time, the management group was not so quick to doubt them.

In addition to the surge in sales, they were seeing a decisive uptick in profits. After they put the finishing touches on the full-year budget, Darcy sent a copy to Bob for his review. That afternoon, she received a call from Bob.

"Darcy," he began, "this budget is a thing of beauty. Do you really think this is possible? Sales up 17 percent and profits up 50 percent?"

"I do, Bob," she answered. "We went through everything line by line. It's by far the most comprehensive budget we have done since I've been here. If anything, I think we are being conservative. Harry's presence in IT Services is beginning to make a big difference. I think he will help us far exceed the benchmarks we had set for ourselves. Also, Elaine and her managers are being very successful in motivating the sales team to produce. That's brought a real energy to the whole company. It just feels different here. Then there is Service: Bryan has had the technicians on the new compensation plan for a few months and service costs are already down 10 percent. My guess is that will continue to fall as the inventory issues get ironed out. Ted is doing a great job in the warehouse getting that done. Even Clint seems to have gotten with the program."

As the core values committee wrapped up their work, Elaine asked to present to the management group at one of the Monday morning meetings. Darcy, Ted, Bryan, and Daryl were especially interested in seeing what the group had come up with. When they walked into the conference room the following Monday, Elaine and her committee were already there set to do their presentation. The marketing department had been working hard to finish the design for the poster, so Elaine had invited Jim to join the group for the presentation. After everyone arrived, Carl, the representative from the service department, began by giving the group an overview of the process the committee went through to come up with their finished product. He said that several employees had contacted them about changes to their initial surveys. Apparently, Daryl's new approach to communication had changed a few minds. When Carl finished, he walked over to the poster and uncovered it. The background was done in the distinctive Burgess Green with the thirtieth anniversary logo as a wallpaper effect. In the middle were the six core values that had been decided on by 60 percent of the company:

1. We check our egos at the door.

2. We are committed to our customers.

3. We listen, we care, we serve.

4. We have open, honest communications.

5. We are a team committed to each other.

6. We have fun.

Carl smiled and said, "The fourth one was a late addition."

Darcy, Ted, Bryan and Daryl looked at each other and smiled. Just a few months ago, they would have never thought that communication would have come close to making the list. They all knew that regaining trust would certainly take longer, but all felt that they were on the right track.

"Well," said Elaine, crossing her arms impatiently, "what do you guys think?"

"I love it," said Betty, "I think those guys are speechless." She pointed toward Darcy, Ted, Bryan, and Daryl.

"Yep," said Bryan, breaking the silence. "Y'all did good."

At that, everyone clapped, and a few walked over to shake Jim's hand.

After the books were closed at year-end, Bob asked Darcy to send Great Ridge updated financial statements. That same afternoon, she received a call from Paul Dugan.

"Darcy," Paul said as she answered the phone. "I got the reports. Very exciting. You guys have really started to turn things around."

"Hi, Paul," she said. "Yes, I must say things are really starting to take off. Everyone is working together so well. We are having a lot of fun."

"Well, that is one of your new core values, isn't it?" he asked. Paul had been closely following Burgess Industries the past few months; the updated core values statement on their website did not get past him.

"Yes," she said, "giving the employees a say in things has really changed the atmosphere. They gave us an honest viewpoint on what it is to work for Burgess."

"Listen, Darcy," Paul said, "I've been meaning to give you a call to see how things are working out with your new controller. Have you had a chance to reduce your hours with Burgess?"

"Funny you should ask. I officially started my consulting contract at the first of the year," said Darcy, a little confused by his questions. "Sheila has been on board for a few months and has taken over most of the day to day duties. I still attend the management meetings and work in the office a few hours each week. I'm doing a lot of work from home, though. I must admit, Paul: it's the best of both worlds."

"Darcy, that's fantastic. Okay, I'm going to cut to the chase. The reason I asked is because I want to hire you to do some work for Great Ridge. We have several dealerships we are looking at, and I need someone with your experience to help Mary with the due diligence. She is becoming a bit overwhelmed. It would require some travel to visit the different locations, but you can do a bulk of the work from home." Darcy paused to collect her thoughts. She honestly could not think of anything she would rather do, but she didn't want to sound overly excited.

"Sounds interesting, Paul", she said. "Why don't we discuss some details?"

"Great," he said, "can you fly to New York next week? We'll sit down with Andrew and Mary and hammer out some details."

"Just give me a date and time. I'll be there," she said.

Almost three years to the day after the "intervention" with Bob, Paul, Darcy, and Daryl sat with Bob in the same conference room to again discuss the future of Burgess Industries. The two full years of financial statements since then had shown double-digit growth. Burgess IT was not only cash flow positive, but was turning a profit. Bob was ready to let go, and Paul was ready to make Bob the offer he was looking for.

Since Darcy had been immersed in the company, Paul felt confident that there would be no surprises. In addition to the strong financial performance, Daryl had spent the last three years building a team on which he could depend. No longer did Burgess rely on one, or even a few, for their success. A net promoter score of 98 percent proved that their reputation was on the rise throughout North Carolina. To further that reputation, they had re-established ties with Burgess Outreach a few months earlier, and had signed on as the major sponsor for the yearly golf tournament. Ron and Janet had turned the charity into something that Bob was especially proud of.

"Bob, are we going to do this?" asked Paul.

"I think so," answered Bob. "It's been quite a ride, but I think I'm finally ready. Darcy assures me that you have no intention of changing anything. You know how important that is to me. I don't want this to negatively affect anyone."

"Don't worry, Bob," said Paul. "Your family is in good hands."

Bob gave him his signature smile. "Where do I sign?"

Darcy thought about the time that had passed since the initial negotiations with Great Ridge. Burgess Industries had become something they were all proud of. She was so happy to have been a part of it.

# EPILOGUE

**Over the course of eight years Darcy** and her team encountered a lot of different common workplace issues. Their experiences and the way they worked together (or didn't) to solve problems provides insight on how similar points of contention in our own workplaces can be avoided and negotiated through. Below is a recap of why the Burgess team faced so many challenges.

## 1. The Importance of Good Communication

A company's culture of communication, good or bad, starts at the top. It was obvious that neither Bob nor Ron realized this. It is so important to set a good example by being as transparent as possible to the entire management team. That team, in turn, needs to communicate well to their employees. The "team" will be a team in name only if there is not an open line of communication. It is uncomfortable and counterproductive to work in an environment where you feel that you are not part of the team. When there are disputes, they are resolved much more quickly in an honest, open environment. In exit interviews, lack of communication is one of the leading reasons ex-employees give for leaving.

## 2. Find a Board of Directors, No Matter How Small You Are

Bob would have been much better served if he had appointed a board of directors to monitor his business when he retired. It doesn't matter how business savvy or how smart someone is; no one person has all the best answers on how to run a company. More and more small business owners are turning to trusted advisors to provide input when working toward attaining their business goals. This network can be very similar to the board of directors that all large companies have, and should consist of people who have, themselves, been successful in business. A board of directors provides a measure of accountability. The board should monitor the financial performance of all business units and be given periodic updates on the business plans and forecasts. Big decisions for the company should always be taken to the board for their input or approval.

## 3. Instead of Searching for the "Magic Bullet," Look Within

It's quite normal for a small businessperson to feel the weight of the world knowing that the livelihood of tens maybe hundreds of families is dependent on you keeping the doors open. When things are not running perfectly it is human nature to go in search of that "Magic Bullet." Ron was reluctant to engage people within the organization to come up with ideas that could have sparked growth. Instead he looked for outside ideas which turned out to be ineffective due to culture, scalability, and market differences. Oftentimes your "Magic Bullet" is right under your nose. You just need to recognize it.

## 4. Micromanaging Will Do Great Damage to Your Company

There was no question that Ron's need to be in total control of every aspect of the organization hampered the company's growth. He lost good employees, and the employees who stayed eventually became useless when they were needed to be relied upon. Many studies have been done on why some people have this need to micromanage. The findings to some degree are surprising. The obvious characteristic is that the person has trust issues. However, beyond that, it goes to a lack of confidence and personal insecurity. If the person controls everything, there is less chance that they will be discovered to be a "fraud." What is ironic is in many cases the classic micromanager sees himself as a great leader, when that could not be farther from the truth.

## 5. Companies Need Strong Managers with Real Authority

While Ron had a group of both experienced managers (Daryl and Darcy) and a burgeoning future leader (Bryan), their skills as managers were not being used effectively because they were given no real authority. As a company grows it is vital to have people with strong management skills to whom you can delegate the running of the different segments of the business. Once those managers are identified and given the title, it is imperative to give them real authority. Managers must be able to make day-to-day decisions regarding their area of the business. There may be times when there isn't agreement on how something was handled, but that should be dealt with in such a way that the manager's authority is not undermined. A manager who is overruled constantly will lose confidence in his abilities and ultimately second guess everything he does. Having a company of managers who can't make basic decisions without consulting with the "powers that be" will reach a point where growth will be completely stifled.

## 6. Budget and Forecast New Business Ventures

Starting a new business venture within your existing unit can be very lucrative and could certainly accelerate the growth of your overall business. However, jumping into a new area just because it is what everyone else is doing is a bad idea unless you first do your homework. This is exactly what Ron did with the managed IT services department. Budgeting for a new business unit requires careful planning, adequate capital, and a thoughtful estimate of revenues and expenses for the foreseeable future. Time and money should be spent on market research, training for employees (especially when moving into an area that is unfamiliar), and branding. New ventures can be structured in different ways which should be thoroughly investigated to determine what is best for your company and market. A failing business unit can suck the life out of an otherwise strong and profitable company.

## 7. If You Move Your Office, Plan, Budget, then Implement

One of the most exciting times for a business is when the current office is outgrown and it's time to move to a bigger—hopefully nicer—space. Along with the excitement there can be a great deal of disruption to the flow of work. One thing is for certain, a move will end up being more involved than anyone originally imagined. This can be minimized with adequate preplanning. For whatever reason, Ron decided to take total control of Burgess's move. Perhaps he thought it would be less disruptive, but it had the opposite effect. It's important to get input from every department on how they feel the move will affect their area, and go to great strides to address those concerns. Not everyone will be equally excited about the big change that is in store. It stands to reason that the owner wants the new office to bear his or her mark. However, if there are key employees who played a part in building the business, it's a good idea to allow their input. They've earned the right to be a part of the creation. Once there is a plan on what to do with the space, and when and how to move with it, it's time to get quotes from vendors and create a budget with a cash flow statement. It is so easy for costs to get out of hand when there are no guidelines. Identifying vendors and setting up accounts will help with cash flow and expense tracking as all expenses will show up on an invoice and payment will most likely have terms.

## 8. Give Multiple People in Your Organization Your Ear

This is especially important for owners like Bob Burgess who are no longer involved in the day-to-day operations of the business. When Bob retired, he had the luxury of not needing to show up every day because he had Ron to run things. This is a wonderful thing, but he became lazy and only relied on Ron's account of what was going on. An owner, even one who is still involved, needs to stay engaged with his workforce. The best way to get an idea of what is really going on in an organization is to have an open dialogue with all employees without fear of retribution. A one-on-one conversation with the manager of each department every month would have been very helpful for Bob. People will be honest, if they know their conversations are private, and their suggestions will be fairly assessed.

## 9. Define Your Organization's Core Values and Walk the Walk

You hear a lot of talk these days about core values and their importance in describing the culture of a business. However, it is also important that the identification of a company's core values be true and sincere. Stating core values for a company and not walking the walk can be counterproductive. Ron wrote what he wanted Burgess's core values to be, but those were not the values that made Burgess a good company even before Bob retired. It was almost as if he was telling his employees "do as I say, not as I do." This is a recipe for bad morale. Much thought must go into a statement of core values. Employee input is critical to the process.

# ABOUT THE AUTHOR

**Ellen McIlhenny** is currently a partner and business transition expert with the consulting firm B2B CFO®, specializing in strategic and business transition planning. She graduated with an accounting degree from Virginia Tech and spent more than twenty years as a CFO or controller in mid-sized and large, privately-held businesses.

As the mother of a child with special needs, Ellen has spent much of her adult life as an advocate for the disabled. This has led her to serve on several state and private non-profit boards of directors.

Her favorite pastimes are writing, golfing, watching her sons play volleyball, and following Hokie sports.

She lives in Montpelier, Virginia with her husband Dennis and their three sons Ben, Woody, and CW.